A. Barrow

Songs of Praise and Practical Life

A. Barrow

Songs of Praise and Practical Life

ISBN/EAN: 9783337181451

Printed in Europe, USA, Canada, Australia, Japan

Cover: Foto ©Lupo / pixelio.de

More available books at **www.hansebooks.com**

Songs of Praise

and Practical Life.

BY A. BARROW.

(Copyright Applied For.)

MARCELINE, MISSOURI.
WALTER CASH, PUBLISHER.
1899.

PREFACE.

The world is full of books, many of them worthless, which have been written purely for speculation. But in writing this little book I hope that a money consideration has had nothing to do with it. My object has been to benefit mankind and for the comfort of all Christians, that they might become more interested in the spiritual life, and be less wrapped up in the things of the world.

But there is a way in which I feel that I have been compensated already, and that is by the strengthening and comforting of my own mind in the consideration of God's love and care for His people. It has helped much in passing my remnant of days, and it occurred to me that if these things were comforting to me they might be to others.

I have written mostly in verse, though I do not claim to be a poet, but I was always a lover of poems. To know what to write, and how to write it, that it might be a benefit to others, has been a trouble to me. Oh! that I might lead some who are burdened to turn and serve the living God. I am persuaded that many of the children of God are swallowed up by the busy world, and have joined themselves to its idols. How to win these back and get them away from their captors has been my study, and my object in writing, for it is a shame for those who have been purged from their sins to continue in disobedience.

As to the worth of this book I must leave that with brethren to judge. I hope to have their prayers, and that we shall meet beyond the shores of time, free from sin.

A. BARROW.

Barrow, Ill.

SONGS OF PRAISE AND PRACTICAL LIFE.

---

1.   C. M.

Am I His Child?

Am I the Lord's own child, and sought
   By grace and love divine?
Am I a child free grace has brought
   From death's dark danger line?

Am I His child? From nature's field,
   In this cold world below,
In satan's clutch, I could not yield—
   Man's worst and hateful foe.

Am I his child? With aching heart,
   My love for nature slain,
Pierced through as with a stinging dart,
   Can I a Savior claim?

Am I a child from sin made free,
   The sin and guilt removed—
All borne away upon the tree—
   Am I a child now loved?

Am I His child, indeed, a son,
    And Christ to me revealed?
Am I His own adopted one?
    From nature's open field?

Am I a child by grace and love,
    By promise sought and found—
And chosen by the Lord above,
    To heaven's mansion bound?

2.   C. M.

Love.

Love is the sweetest flower that grows
    From life's immortal tree,
And every gentle wind that blows,
    Its sweetness wafts to me.

Rich, pure and spotless, clothed in white,
    Its velvet leaves like gold,
The fairest flower that ever bloomed—
    Its beauty can't be told.

Entwined around with healing leaves,
    A balm for every wound,
'Tis borne along on every breeze,
    A cordial gladly found.

'Tis onward bound from life's fair tree,
    At every table spread,
And wafted forth o'er land and sea,
    Alive, and never dead.

'Tis like the dewdrop from on high,
    Upon the tender vine,

The purest blossom from the sky—
  Oh! may I claim it mine.

It clusters round a brother's breast,
  And draws us near to him;
The binding tie that brings us rest—
  Undying love within.

It is a welcome, lovely guest,
  That never brings us harm,
So richly clothed with grace and blessed,
  It brings us no alarm.

Its perfect beauty far outshines
  The sweetest scented rose;
Along the great, strong wheels of time
  It onward, constant, goes.

O, let us court its ways to learn,
  Its joys, may they ours be,
And may we drink of love divine,
  From life's immortal tree.

3.   C. M.

Sea of Sin.

Between us and the spirit world
  There is a troubled sea;
None can escape its hungry waves,
  Or from its presence flee

Great rolling clouds of sin arise,
  With stains of crimson hue,
And spread far out before our eyes,
  While we are passing through.

We faintly see a glimmering light
　　While moving with the tide,
But many woes our hopes to blight,
　　Are found on every side.

Oh! what a fearful, dismal way
　　Is ours, in this great plain;
So many things to lead astray,
　　While we would heaven gain.

Yet on we go, and onward still,
　　O'er this tempestuous sea;
We journey much against our will,
　　In spite of every plea.

Approaching dangers make us shrink
　　From a dark and loathsome grave,
As we often feel that we shall sink
　　Beneath the boisterous wave.

Our only hope is that our God,
　　Through Christ will calm this sea,
And still the raging, swelling flood,
　　And set our spirits free.

4.　　　　　　　　　　　　　　　C. M.
Thy Way.

O may we learn Thy way, O Lord,
　　With humble hearts of prayer,
Obey and cherish every word—
　　Our love to center there.

O may we dwell where thou dost stay,
　　With peace and love be crowned,

That we may walk in Thine own way—
    With Jesus Christ be found.

So often in the dark we roam,
    In slippery paths are found;
We cannot claim this world our home,
    We're on uncertain ground.

Our lives are slowly ebbing low,
    Our race is quickly run;
And onward to the goal we go
    With every rising sun.

The going down of life appears
    At every turning day,
The swift approach of turning years,
    Of life's fast fading way.

There is a land beyond this vale,
    No mortal man hath trod,
A promised land for the redeemed,
    A rest, a home with God.

5.   S. M.

Jesus Our Savior.

Have we no God to fear?
    No Father to obey?
No parent's love to us so dear,
    To drive our fears away?

Have we no Christ to love—
    Our Father's gift to men?
'Twas He, the pure one from above,
    Was crucified for sin.

Did Israel's King arise,
   From lowly Bethlehem spring,
Ascend in glory to the skies,
   Triumphant Priest and King?

Love, faith and life begun.
   In all his children dwell,
Secured and saved through his dear Son,
   Who doeth all things well.

The Prince of life was slain
   For some—I hope for me—
His children's sins were on him lain,
   He bore them on the tree.

His blood, there shed by men,
   The earth and rocks did stain;
He gave His life for every sin,
   That they might heaven gain.

Then let us join and sing
   Of Jesus from above,
Our hope, our joy, our Priest and King,
   Our Savior whom we love.

6.   C. M.

The Heavenly Home.

It might have been a wandering thought,
   Or just in vision's dream,
My mind was made to soar aloft
   And view the heavenly plain.

Great armies of the upper skies
   In glittering, bright array,

In dazzling beauty to my eyes,
  In one vast field did lay.

They came like melting drops of rain,
  Descending from above,
And then ascended whence they came,
  To realms of endless love.

What joy it gives to fainting hearts,
  To know there is a heaven,
A blissful rest which love imparts,
  To all who are forgiven.

C. M.

Heavenly Canaan.

There is a land of living streams,
  A fountain opened wide;
A ray of light forever beams
  Across death's chilling tide.

No beating storms nor howling wind,
  Nor raging seas that roar,
No poisonous stains from worldly sins,
  Can reach that blissful shore.

No mountains tall or valleys deep,
  Or mighty hills are there,
Nor rivers long where monsters creep,
  On Canaan's plains so fair.

No brazen walls of sin are there,
  No tempting snares are found;
But favored children from afar,
  From all the world around.

There's no broad river there to cross,
   No gallant ships go by,
No sons and daughters to be lost,
   Nor children's fainting cry.

The crooked ways are all made straight,
   And roughest places plain,
And once inside our Father's gate,
   Forever we'll remain.

A healing balm of mercy flows
   From fountains opened wide,
And love is gushing from the streams,
   To all the world outside.

It is a land of endless rest,
   The humble Christian's home,
With mansions bright for every guest,
   Where ransomed children come.

8.   L. M.

Religion.

Religion brings us sweet relief
From all our cares, and toils, and grief;
It soothes and calms the sinner's breast,
'Tis there he finds the sweetest rest.

Religion gives us love and peace,
All doubt and fear is made to cease;
It is religion from above
That fills our souls with joy and love.

It is religion hope imparts,
And gladdens all our fainting hearts;

'Tis all of God and his free grace,
That teaches us our rightful place.

How poor the hopes which on works rely,
'Tis God's free grace prepares to die;
It is the power of God's own hand
That fits us for the heavenly land.

9. 　　　　　　　　　　　　　　L. M.
Flesh and Blood.

We've flesh and blood around us wound,
　Its fettering bands all made complete,
And in these homes are closely bound,
　Without obtaining our consent.

'Tis wondrous strange, but still 'tis true,
　Entombed in clay as now you see;
'Tis wondrous strange—a mystery—
　How nature's children came to be.

But such are we in life's abode,
　Awhile, at least, here to remain,
Here on this fast revolving globe,
　Are changing, yet are still the same.

When called from this poor house of clay,
　In which we groan while here below,
We'll humbly bow to God's own way,
　Submissive and resigned to go.

No polar waves, nor sultry suns,
　Can ever reach us, except here;
And this short race we soon shall run,
　From earth we shortly disappear.

Now those who travel in this way
    And realize their certain fate—
Their bodies in the ground must lay—
    Should call on God before too late

I'm not ashamed to own Him now,
    Before the world on Him to call;
Before the world I make this vow,
    I'll call on God and pray for all.

For me 'tis best to live this way,
    For I can be more reconciled—
Do all I can, on every day,
    If I am God's, or am His child.

10.   C. M.

Experience.

Wilt Thou, O Lord, remember me,
    Poor, helpless and defiled?
For from thy wrath, O Lord, I'd flee,
    A sinner found with guile.

I fain would leave this sinful world,
    Below the beasts would be;
I'm tossed along this busy whirl,
    O Lord, remember me.

I cast my eys across the land,
    Behold! I look and see
Great heaps of sin before me stand—
    O Lord, remember me.

An open grave before me lies,
    From this I cannot flee—

My wicked way is so despised—
  O Lord, remember me.

I would repent and turn to God,
  Would make no other plea,
And travel o'er a smoother road,
  If Thou'dst remember me.

But in this world of sin and crime,
  My nature doth agree;
Could I but claim some promise mine!
  Dear Lord, remember me.

I'd cast my traffic at my feet,
  From filty rags be free,
And some new way or promise greet—
  O Lord, remember me.

The light breaks forth and I exclaim,
  O God, how can it be,
That though so vile, so prone to sin,
  Thou hast remembered me?

In a new field I love to roam,
  Where living trees I see,
Are sending forth their rich perfume,
  And feel Thou remember'st me.

They send their fragrance far away,
  And waft their sweets to Thee,
All guided by the Spirit's sway—
  The Lord remember'st me.

Remembers this poor, dying worm,
  Once blind, but now can see—

When in the cold and wintry storm,
　The Lord remembered me.

O surely God to me was kind,
　By His own Son to free,
From every taint of sin inclined—
　He has remembered me

Oh! had I power my voice to raise,
　For what He's done for me,
Half high enough to sound His praise,
　In Christ remembering me.

11.　　　　　　　　　　　　　　　P. M.
The Church's Invitation.
(TUNE, "FATHERLAND.")

There is a place where the saints are led,
　A city of friendship and love,
The banqueting house where all are fed,
　Whose hopes are all centered above.

CHORUS:
Come to this place with your harps of gold,
　Come join in this fellowship band,
Come to this place with heart and soul,
　And live in this beautiful land.

Come to this place for the Lord is here,
　And drink from the cup he will give,
Come drink from the rock, the water is clear,
　O come, and his blessings receive.

CHO.—

Come to this place for a home to dwell,
  And rest with the flock here at noon;
Come feed with the lambs who fare so well,
  For all earth's pleasures are gone.
Cho.—

Come to this place, there is always room,
  Where the vine with its clusters are green,
A welcome place, where all may come,
  And trees in their beauty are seen.
Cho.—

Come to this place with your lamps all trimmed,
  Reflecting their beautiful light,
O come, with your psalms and hymns to sing,
  Expressing your rapturous delight.
Cho.—

Come to this place, where we love to tell,
  To the strangers and pilgrims of God,
Of the homes of their friends we love so well,
  A palace with mansions of love.
Cho.—

12.   C. M.
Free Grace.

O let us sing of grace divine,
  And give our Father praise
For all his glorious gifts sublime,
  The wonders of his ways.

O let us sing redeeming grace,
  The wonders from above,

The smilings of our Father's face
  Revealed to us in love.

O let us sing of grace, and trust
  Our Father's gentle care;
Beneath the shadow of his wings,
  Our hopes all center there.

O let us sing of God's free grace,
  His goodness and His love,
O let us of his riches taste,
  So freely from above.

O let us sing of grace divine.
  With humble hearts rejoice,
A world of sinners saved by grace,
  Our Father's own free choice.

13.   C. M.
Gift of Love.

The dearest, richest gift of God,
  The priceless gem of love,
That thaws the cold and frozen heart,
  Descending from above.

On angel wings is borne to earth,
  And melts the hearts of stone,
It brings the wandering strangers forth.
  And guides the travelers home.

How pure and peaceful are its ways,
  Life's fairest, sweetest flower,
Rich streams of love end all our days,
  And still the passing hour.

The bud once planted in the heart,
    Its gentle growth is seen,
Its healing leaves and fruit impart,
    Brought forth in living green.

'Tis not a jewel bought and sold
    By slight and skill of men,
Its fragrance, sweet and rich, flows out,
    A welcome guest within.

A living plant that never dies,
    It fills our hearts aglow,
'Twill ripen in the upper skies—
    This tender plant below.

It kindles in the Christian's breast,
    And brings the sweetest peace;
It brings a sweet and quiet rest,
    Has endless stores of grace.

Descending from the courts above
    This binding tie is given,
And onward to fair Canaan's land,
    Returns again to heaven.

14.   C. M.

The Stream of Love.

Beneath the glorious throne of God,
    Behold an ocean's stream,
And flowing from the realm above,
    Its waters brightly gleam.

It spreads abroad to every land,
    And brings the weary rest,

'Tis sending forth its healing balm,
  On all the kindred blest.

'Tis sweetened with a Savior's love,
  Whose flowing streams supply,
And on his precious, cleansing blood,
  Poor sinners must rely.

To every sick and wounded soul,
  Its healing waters flow,
'Tis reaching them at every shoal,
  In all the world below.

It gently soothes their aching breasts,
  And while its waters gleam,
'Tis bringing them the sweetest rest,
  From this broad ocean's stream.

15.   C M.

This Dreary Life.

How sad this dreary life appears,
  When thinking of the past,
The rugged ways and tempting snares,
  And drifting time so fast.

How dark and lonesome is the way,
  On all this journey through,
We could not wish to longer stay,
  Or ask the hours more slow.

No gladsome field of joy and mirth,
  Should long entice us here,
The bitter pangs upon this earth,
  Are widespread, everywhere.

When death's much dreaded hour arrives,
    And we must launch away,
May our departing souls arise
    To climes of endless day.

Shine forth in dazzling garments bright,
    In realms that ne'er shall cease,
Revealed to us on death's dark night,
    A life of joy and peace.

When joined to that bright throne above,
    Where saints have come before,
With angels there in endless love,
    Where sorrows are no more.

16.   C. M.
The Way, The Truth and The Life.

Do I possess an honest heart?
    O Lord, I cannot say;
A poor, despised and wicked one,
    Am I a castaway?

Behold! O God, and look within,
    And view the carnal mind,
So destitute and so unclean,
    But little hope can find.

O Lord, I mourn and weep and sigh,
    My inward sin reveal,
How can I be prepared to die—
    My wickedness conceal?

Here in this gloomy, doubting mind,
    My lonesome days roll on,

And many groans and tears are mine,
  O Lord, shall I despond?

How sad it seems from day to day,
  Not knowing what I be,
The time, it speeds so fast away,
  Such little light I see.

O Lord, our God, I humbly pray,
  Do hear my tender cry,
Do lift, O God, the clouds away,
  Prepare us all to die.

Through Christ, the Lord, we'll gain the day,
  With rapture and delight;
Through Christ, the Lord, the only way—
  The Way, the Truth, the Life.

17.   11s.

Last Farewell.
(WRITTEN DURING SICKNESS.)

Farewell, my dear brethren, I bid all adieu,
Death's gate stands wide open, and I'm passing
    through;
Do hear me, I pray thee, and list to my song,
My trials I'll tell you while traveling along.

In chains of affliction and trouble I'm bound,
Distresses and sorrows I always have found;
A wayfaring stranger on earth's wide domain,
'Midst woes and confusion, in grief and in pain.

Dear brethren, I leave you in this dreary land,
Be patient in waiting your Savior's commands;

Come wealth with its pleasures, the best that befall,
To live in His kingdom is greater than all.

O be not discouraged, though your number be few,
Meet often together, your bright hopes renew;
The Jews, they were fewer than the nations around,
But God's love was among them, and always there found.

To the care-worn and weary, and feeble ones, too,
In the spirit of love always found to be true;
Though foes and afflictions oppress you below,
Your home's up in heaven, well guarded you know.

Dear brethren, be faithful in truth and in love,
Live in peace with each other, be kind as the Dove,
Assisting your preacher, help him on his way,
And bear with each other, for each other pray.

I cannot help crying while I write you this song,
But hope again to meet you—it cannot be long—
In mansions above where we ever will sing,
With loud hallelujahs sweet heaven will ring.

I bid you farewell, I shall meet you no more
When meeting together on this earthly shore;

But if we are suffered to meet up above,
We'll join there in singing of God's wondrous love.

There sing with each other in that cloudless sky,
There'll be no more parting, every eye will be dry;
I bid you farewell, till we meet over there,
Where the sun's always shining, the sky always clear.

13.   C. M.
Star of Bethlehem.

There is a sweet and healing balm,
    A living, cleansing stream;
'Tis flowing from the atoning Lamb,
    The star of Bethlehem.

Yes, unto us a child is born,
    A Son most freely given,
The mighty God the earth adorns,
    The Prince of Life from heaven.

He, too, was clothed with flesh and blood,
    This fair One from on high,
The Spirit like a snow white dove,
    Descending from the sky.

This is God's well beloved Son,
    In whom He is well pleased,
The church of Christ on earth begun,
    We cannot be deceived.

He bought the field with His own blood,
    And sought a precious pearl,
He gave His life, redeemed to God
    A dark and sinful world.

With heavy seals in death was laid,
    Confined in Joseph's tomb,
He broke the bars of death and fled,
    Left angels in His room.

'Tis by his stripes that we are healed,
    Our sins all borne away,
And those who love, believe and feel,
    Should all His laws obey.

O let us look by faith to Him,
    Who washed us white as snow,
And trust the star of Bethlehem
    To conquer every foe.

19.   C. M.

A Prisoner.

For many years a prisoner bound,
    But not in stocks and chains,
Nor bound in dungeons underground,
    Nor scourged with stripes and pains.

But in the bonds of flesh and blood,
    A trembling heart within,
All nature like a trembling flood—
    A prisoner bound in sin.

Herein we groan day after day,
    And seek relief to find,

Some safe escape from nature's way,
    To free the burdened mind.

We grope inside this fleshly wall
    And strive to conquer sin,
Not knowing when the house must fall,
    And free the man within.

Enclosed within this temporal home,
    Where dwelleth no good thing,
Our only hope from Christ must come,
    By Him the gate will swing.

We wait with patience for that day,
    The trumpet will sound loud,
The gate swing open all the way,
    And we'll go home to God.

We'll bid farewell to every foe,
    To that which bound us fast,
We'll bid farewell to all below,
    Heaven's rest will find at last.

20.   L. M.

Born Again.

The carnal mind, or natural man,
Cannot discern God's righteous plan,
Till life springs up, reveals the way,
Directs his thoughts, his works display.

Life comes to man just like the wind,
Disclosing all his inward sin;
The heart prepared, a willing mind,
God's spirit never fails to find.

They turn from darkness to the light,
Translated freely from the night;
The cruel mockings of his God,
Are changed to fear the chastening rod.

The natural man, he changeth not,
Nor worldly pleasures hath forgot,
Still craves and thirsts for worldly food,
Desires again the same old road.

Now in a strait betwixt the two—
The cruel world seems well to do,
With malice, hatred, sin beguiled;
But Christ steps in and saves the child.

All forms and fashions fade away,
Desires new form day by day,
And nature seems to lose her power,
While grace is growing every hour.

The strongest power holds fast the field—
The weaker in the end must yield—
Free grace and love now manifest
A child of mercy, ever blest.

O what a happy thought, to know
That God has always loved us so;
While drinking down the cup of sin,
He takes control and reigns within.

Prepares the heart, directs the tongue,
Engages the mind in psalms of song,
And guides the traveler by His grace,
The footsteps of His flock to trace.

21.   C M.
The Grave.

What if our bodies fade and die—
  Lay in the silent tomb!
Beneath the shady trees all lie,
  This is their certain doom.

They'll sweetly sleep low in the ground,
  In death's cold arms be laid,
The earth will hide them from the storm,
  Till they shall rise again.

The pale, white-sheeted nations rest,
  With millions of the past,
Down in the cold and lonesome earth,
  To await the trumpet's blast.

There is a great, immortal King,
  In heaven's glorious land,
Who will the sleeping dust all bring,
  Before Him all must stand.

He'll take the righteous in His arms,
  And cast the bad away,
He'll claim the righteous for his own,
  And for the heavenly day.

22.   C M.
His Name.

The precious name of our dear Lord,
  Let saints all gladly tell;
Although the world rejects His word,
  He is Immanuel.

The precious name of our dear Lord,
  O let us all proclaim,
And shout the victory through his Son,
  That dear and sacred name.

The precious name of our dear Lord!
  Let all the world rejoice,
The suffering, bleeding Son of God,
  The dead shall hear his voice.

The precious name of our dear Lord—
  Come guilty souls who fear—
Come praise, adore and glorify,
  And wipe away each tear.

23. C. M.
Help Us to Pray.

For wicked sinners, poor and vile,
  We bow in humble prayer,
We're at thy feet, O God of power,
  Our pleadings are sincere.

O grant us, Lord, sustaining grace,
  O give us more and more,
O guide our feet in every place,
  Along this sinful shore.

O feed our souls with grace divine,
  And give us drink from heaven,
May we improve each hour of time
  That to us here is given.

O if Thou lovest us, help us pray,
  O help us do Thy will,

To follow in the lowly way,
  Thy pleasures to fulfill.

O guard us, guide us in the truth,
  And be our staff and shield,
That we may not Thy way forsake,
  And not to satan yield.

O hear us, Lord, to Thee we cry,
  O drive our fears away,
Draw near, O Lord, for Thee we sigh,
  Do help us pray today.

O help us live for Thee alone,
  Do help us, Lord, along,
O help us pray, Almighty One,
  And help us, Lord, with song.

24.   C. M.

The City of God.

O can I walk the golden streets,
  Or view the promised land?
O can I taste the heavenly sweets,
  Or among the righteous stand?

Can I, O Lord, prepare to die?
  Or reconcile the mind?
O can I from these regions fly,
  And greater pleasures find?

Can I, O Lord, from troubles flee,
  And leave them all below?
Can I, O Lord, from them go free,
  And sweeter riches know?

O can I bathe my soul in peace
    Beyond this fading shore?
O can I reach that heavenly place
    Where sorrows are no more?

Where fears of torment are unknown,
    Destructions gate will close,
The Shepherd will his sheep all own.
    And drive away their foes.

'Tis sweet to think of such a place,
    A land of pure delight,
A realm, a stream of love can trace,
    And where there is no night.

O can I reach those heavenly fields,
    Or walk the golden street,
With Jasper walls and gates of pearl,
    Where saints immortal meet?

25.   C. M.
Before the Church.

Once more before the Lord we stand,
    With trembling and with fear,
With our poor, stammering, lisping tongue,
    Before the saints appear.

We ask God's help while struggling on,
    To understand His word,
That truth and knowledge shine upon
    The servants of the Lord.

We stand with fear, O Lord, today,
    All tired, faint and worn,

Before Thee bow and ask the way,
   O guide our words and tongue.

We ask for light to know Thy will,
   From Thee and Thee alone,
All Thy desire we would fulfill,
   Disclaiming all our own.

26.   C. M.
Free Grace.

We see Thy marks beneath the sky,
   O God of earth and heaven,
O can we not on thee rely,
   And praise for comfort given.

The silent winds obey Thy voice,
   And shake the withering tree;
Just so with man, 'twas not his choice,
   But grace that made him free.

'Tis grace that moves and shines upon
   Poor sinners in disguise;
'Tis grace that leads them safely on,
   And grace their works despise.

'Tis grace that teaches us to pray,
   And grace that feeds our souls;
Free grace provides the sinner's way,
   'Tis grace that makes us whole.

O if we ask of Him more grace,
   With faith and hope and love,
He will not turn away His face,
   But feed us from above.

27.
A Poor, Weary Traveler.

The pale horse and his rider
　Are knocking at my door;
The voice of death is calling,
　I'm not deceived, I'm sure;
I am packing up for traveling,
　Putting on my best attire,
To court the Lord's affections
　Is my whole heart's desire.

CHORUS:

　O I'm poor and weary, tired and needy,
　　Poor and weary on the way,
　O I'm poor and weary, tired and needy,
　　Poor and weary on the way.

O I know I am poor and needy,
　My apparel doth not shine,
It is common and unfitting,
　Not princely, nor made fine;
'Tis cloth of my own making,
　The best that I can do,
It is poor enough I'm certain,
　Unbecoming and untrue.

CHO.—

'Tis not possessed of beauty,
　All faded out and worn,
Not lasting or enduring,
　All comeliness is shorn;

But I'll answer to his calling,
   With my bundle in my hand,
Though He my works rejecting,
   Nothing's left at my command.

Cho —

But He that sends the pale horse,
   And gives commands to go,
Will send the shining garments,
   They'll be fitting, too, you know;
My feet be shod with sandals,
   In costly garments clad,
Go on the way rejoicing,
   Neither destitute nor sad.

Cho.—

The One who sends the pale horse,
   Conducting me along,
Rejecting my apparel,
   All filthy rags disown,
He will land me up in heaven,
   In garments Jesus wove,
All whole and woven seamless,
   For all His Father's loved.

Cho.—

28.

God's People.

I love God's people, love their ways,
   I love each smiling face,
I love the people that believe
   Salvation's all of grace.

I love them, for they love the Lord,
  And love His truth so well;
I love them, for they love His word,
  And love his truth to tell.

I love the people who depend
  On Jesus Christ for all,
O may I love them to the end,
  And may they never fall.

I love God's people, good and true,
  I love them all as one,
I love them, yes, I know I do,
  Who love the Father's Son.

I love God's people here below,
  Who for the faith contend,
I love them all, the sinners, too,
  I love the sinner's Friend.

I love the poor, afflicted ones,
  Upon this sinful shore,
I love the called and chosen sons,
  I love God's humble poor.

29. C. M.
Lift Us Up.

O lift us up, who pray, O God,
  Some guardian angel send,
O lift us up and be our guard,
  And guide us to the end.

O lift us up from this poor world
Of lust and pride and form,

Deliver us, we pray, O God.
    And keep us from all harm.

O lift us up from this dark night,
    And give us strength and zeal,
That we may fight the Lord's good fight,
    And nothing bad conceal.

Drop down, O God, from thy bright throne,
    Thy fairest drops of grace,
That light may shine both far and near,
    And lighten every place.

30.   C. M.
Pilgrims in the World.

The night is dark, the day is cold,
    Here in this lonesome vale,
Gross darkness spreading o'er the earth,
    Like some strong, sweeping gale.

In meditation, deep in thought,
    Our minds in prayer are led
For poor, lost sinners on this earth,
    Who in their sins are dead.

Behold the masses like a stream,
    In maddening fury fly,
While earthly toys all like a dream,
    Are rushing swiftly by.

With hearts all seared, like iron hard,
    In fleshly deeds of crime,
And not one word for Christ is heard,
    In all this wicked clime.

The dead should bury their own dead,
  Let saints forsake their throng,
Be not by their enticements led,
  Nor captured by their song.

O, if you feel your sins forgiven,
  Through Christ's atoning blood,
Awake, poor sinner, go toward heaven,
  Work for the church of God.

31.   C. M.
Gloom of Death.

Death hangs just like a gloomy pall
  So oft before my eyes;
Its flying messenger may call,
  While we're in tears and sighs.

We're found within this clay and dust,
  Our temporal home on earth,
Although so weak and frail at best,
  And of such little worth.

We still would dwell within this home,
  And suffer on with pain,
We cannot tell just what might come,
  So we would here remain.

But while the fickle light shall burn,
  And time shall hold us here,
O may God's Holy Spirit learn,
  And teach us not to fear.

But when the way seems dark and cold,
  And doubts obscure the day,

The flying messenger may call
   And drive all doubts away.

Surrounded with a host of friends,
   To bid a last good-bye,
When but a thread of life suspends,
   On God we must rely.

32.   C. M.
Let Love Be Ours.

Come sickness, sorrow, pain and death,
   With all their restless hours,
When we shall breathe our latest breath,
   O then, let love be ours.

Our quivering lips and limbs give way,
   Our yielding forms are bent,
O how we moan and groan and pray,
   And ask to be content.

The more we view our life that's past,
   We wonder with surprise
That God would grant us faith at last,
   To gain the heavenly prize.

There's not a single ray of light,
   Comes through the grace of man,
And not one single hope in sight,
   Save Jesus' righteous plan.

O may it be our lot in death,
   That grace may claim the hours,
That when we breathe our latest breath,
   O then let love be ours.

33. L. M.

God's Banner of Love.

God's loving banner first unfurled,
And wrapped around a sinning world.
Its gentle folds around us cast,
Our title to heaven was then made fast.

His laws were given from above,
With this fair emblem of His love;
His power and love—the two combined—
Can never fail each child to find.

A ransom price for man was made,
Before his form in dust was laid;
God can control all things we know,
And save His children here below.

He's not confined by metes and bounds,
Nor standing on uncertain grounds;
This world forever in His sight,
Both through the day and through the night.

His love embraces all around,
And on His banner's always found;
We fell away through pride and lust,
But now love God, who first loved us.

34. L. M.

Bear Us Away.

O come, dear Savior, with a shout,
O come, dear Master, bear us out,
O take Thy wandering children home,
O come, Lord Jesus, Savior, come.

Our loving Savior, faithful Friend,
O may we claim Thee to the end;
O may we meet Him in the air,
O let this be our daily prayer.

With faith and hope and love combined,
He'll bear us all to heaven's clime;
O let us trust in God's dear Son,
Until our earthly race is run.

We'll stand unshaken at our post—
If we're in Christ we'll not be lost;
And in His fullness we shall dwell,
And of his glory love to tell.

He'll bear us on His wings of love,
And take us to our home above;
We'll sail with Him up in the air
To that sweet clime all bright and fair.

There bathe our souls in perfect peace,
In that fair world of endless rest;
There'll be no mixtures with alloy,
But we shall have eternal joy.

35.   C. M.

Departed Ones.

Farewell, farewell, dear one, farewell,
   We bid a last adieu;
Thy comeliness we now would tell,
   Thy face we cannot view.

A vacant chair we now behold,
   A corner desolate.

But heaven's mansions now enfold
    The loved ones here of late.

No mortal tongue need undertake
    To paint that heavenly clime,
No mortal tongue could here relate
    How bright its beauties shine.

While we are left behind to mourn
    The dear, departed one,
The spirit flies to yonder world,
    To endless glory's gone.

O Lord, do reconcile our mind,
    And give us peaceful rest,
That we may follow on to find
    A perfect union blessed.

36.
Waiting for the Promised Land.

We have been waiting by the Jordan,
    Many long and weary days,
We are waiting by the river,
    'Neath the sun's reflecting rays;
We have clambered up the mountain,
    We have viewed the promised land,
There beyond the cold, dark river,
    Where the saints immortal stand.

CHORUS:

    We are waiting by the river,
        For our Captain's gone before,

We are waiting to cross over,
  To that bright, celestial shore.

We are gazing on with wonder,
  As we look beyond the stream,
We are only few in number,
  And the Jordan lies between;
But we are going to our fathers—
  Moses, Aaron. Abraham—
We are gathering at the river,
  Waiting for the promised land.

Cho.—

We are sailing across the ocean,
  Full of sorrow, full of pain,
But will soon reach the glad haven,
  And eternal rest will gain;
We are waiting for our Captain,
  With His banner in His hand,
And we'll follow cross the Jordan,
  And will reach the promised land.

Cho.—

We are waiting for the morrow,
  For the coming jubilee,
We are waiting for King Jesus,
  All His angels we shall see;
We are waiting and rejoicing,
  Our deliverance is at hand,
We will leave the world behind us,
  And will reach the promised land.

Cho.—

We are waiting for the morning,
   For the dawning of the day,
When the armies will cross over,
   And will see the shining way;
We'll then meet with saints in heaven,
   And will walk the golden strand,
At the home of our dear Savior,
   When we reach the promised land.

Cho.—

37.   C. M.

The World.

This world has gone away from me,
   And left we far behind;
With it my soul did not agree,
   Its pleasures sought to find.

The world is on a race for wealth,
   All after dumb, false idols go;
Men care not for their lives nor health,
   This world is all they know.

I once along with them did walk,
   And sometimes I would run,
And of their riches loved to talk,
   I loved the busy hum.

Their wealth and pride I did admire,
   With all their fickle charm,
To fill my soul was my desire,
   In their deceitful arms.

But oh! a great and woeful change
　To my poor soul was brought,
Another field I loved to range,
　Another life I sought.

I found my life was burning out,
　And drawing to a close,
And my poor soul was moved about,
　And sought a still repose.

Thank God! I'm not now in the race,
　Nor in this temporal strife,
But He who guides me by His grace,
　Has shown the better life.

38.　　　　　　　　　　　　　　C. M.
The Suffering Gate.

We dread to pass death's suffering gate,
　Its cold and icy gloom,
But lo! the holy angels wait
　To bear us to our home.

Our fainting, failing bodies lie,
　Lose all their strength and power,
The cold and clammy form must die,
　In that sad, trying hour.

O hark, a still, sweet voice is heard,
　Beyond this icy plain,
Be still, and listen to the word—
　The dead shall live again

Poor, fallen man shall rise again,
　And live beyond this vale,

And in that world there is no pain,
   Where life shall never fail.

Cheer up, poor drooping, trembling soul.
   Fear not death's suffering gate,
For while you're passing through its doors,
   The angel throng will wait.

They'll bear you safely on their wings,
   To fairer worlds above,
Where all the heavenly hosts will sing,
   Of God's redeeming love.

39.   L. M.

The Carnal Mind.

What of the mind? How can it be
Both calm and pure and always free
To sleep and slumber when it please,
To be composed and quite at ease?

What of the mind? How can we tell
When on the good or bad may dwell?
How many changes come today?
How much or little it may say?

The thoughts that come and onward go,
We know not how nor why 'tis so;
But would control and hold the mind
Upon the pure when bad's inclined.

We try to turn our minds away
From evil words we thought to say,
But in a moment they arise,
The wicked ones we so despise.

We're always thus, so much perplexed,
Control of the mind so often lose;
We'd place our minds on things we choose,
But they so often will refuse.

One moment we are like a child,
A moment more are almost wild;
Our thoughts gone off in reckless waste,
So often turn to our distaste.

How strange it is we can't control
The carnal mind, nor save the soul,
Nor place our thoughts and hold them there,
From rambling round most everywhere.

We feel our guilt, our minds depraved,
By grace alone can we be saved!
But let us teach the denying school,
And try again ourselves to rule.

Unless we do, we'll leave a spot,
Another page of life to blot;
And thus we try and try again,
Both try and hope, but all in vain.

We often try to change our will,
And often find it unchanged still;
The same old route it loves to go,
And often sinks down deep below.

We'll try and guard the safety line,
To hold it pure throughout our time,
On things we know are for the best,
And trust in God to give the rest.

40.   L M.

The Kingdom Shall Stand.

Nations, like men, are born to die,
   Lose all their power and princely trust;
Kingdoms and monarchs all must lie,
   Crumbled and mingled with the dust.

The earthly kingdoms all sink down,
   Their royal splendor fades away;
The kings and princes lose their crown,
   Their light shines only for a day.

There's only one great sovereign King
   Whose kingdom will forever stand;
His subjects are all chosen men,
   From sea to sea, from land to land.

All nations bow before this One,
   And render homage to His power;
His will on earth, it must be done,
   None can escape their trying hour,

41.   L. M.

Way-side Sinner's Lamentation.

All we poor pilgrims of the dust,
   Are traveling through a misty world;
There's none that's righteous, none are just,
   We're swift along life's pathway hurled.

We're dead in trespass and in sin,
   How shall we meet an angry God?
We've wandered far away from him,
   And now must meet the chastening rod.

We all feel guilty and distressed,
    Afflictions daily do arise,
That mar our peace and happiness,
    Regret with pain and weeping eyes.

Away from God in sin we lie,
    While death's dark door is drawing near,
We shudder and we draw a sigh,
    The fearful night doth now appear.

We're dead in trespass and in sin,
    All we, like sheep, have gone astray;
Some other folds found pasture in,
    Refused our Master to obey.

Our way looks dark and drear to us,
    All worn and tired beneath the sky;
And shall we cross the dismal gulf,
    With dark forebodings from on high?

Fain would we reach the heavenly shore,
    Without the suffering and the pain;
But oh! who then would us restore,
    Or say, The dead shall live again.

Could we but climb the golden stair,
    Without the cross our Savior bore,
And reach that shining world all fair—
    For this the heart and soul implore.

But when we reach death's iron gate,
    And feel its rough-edged hinges swing,
Oh, if it only would but wait!
    We've nothing in our hands to bring.

With death's cold chill upon our face,
   The candle lit, but now grown dim,
We're some of Adam's guilty race
   Who fell outside the path of sin.

But O, dear Lord, is this our doom,
   To slumber low beneath the clay?
We're falling, crumbling to the touch,
   And can't resist, no, not one day.

With wishful hearts we beg the prize,
   God's love and mercy to embrace,
With white-winged angels to arise;
   We ask, O where is God's free grace?

We all fall back with fear, and shrink,
   The pale, white-sheeted nations shun;
The bitter cup we would not drink,
   From death's dark, lonely gate would run.

Lord, reconcile our fainting minds,
   And strip us of self-righteous power,
That we may look by faith to find
   Free grace in that last trying hour.

Then dropping down may rise again,
   With wings immortal soar above,
To life that's free from wayside sin—
   A calm repose, sweet home of love.

And now we feel almost secure,
   And trust in God's free grace again,
We'll trust in him, all pain endure,
   And look beyond for a peaceful reign.

42. 7s. 7s.

Spiritual Family.

A few, but faithful family,
    All o'er this wide domain,
Sought out and led most gently,
    By the gospel's loud proclaim,

CHORUS:

    We will praise our Savior,
        For drawing all to Him,
    We will praise our Redeemer,
        Who saved us all from sin.

Abroad among the nations,
    Poor travelers o'er this land,
Poor, sad and weary children,
    By faith alone they stand.

CHO.—

Strange life of sin and sorrow,
    Not knowing what they be,
Or where they'll be tomorrow,
    Just drifting with the stream.

CHO.—

A faithful band of pilgrims,
    How strong they seem to be,
And trusting all in Jesus,
    Who died for you and me.

CHO.—

Oh! come and join our members,
    For we are homeward bound,

Just waiting our deliverance,
  This world is not our home.

Cho.—

  We soon shall cross death's river,
    That cold and angry stream,
  We'll praise the Lord, the giver,
    For calling all to Him.

Cho.—

43.   P. M.

The Young.

The young, the mirthful and the proud,
Will soon be wrapped in death's cold shroud,
Their worldly pleasure all be o'er,
Soon they will leave this earthly shore.

Chorus:

  O come, dear child, just as you are,
  Come to Jesus and prepare.

Oh! could I but instruct your mind,
With words of love and friendship kind,
To shun the evil snares around,
In every place where they are found.

Cho.—

Oh! will you not to Jesus fly,
Without money come and buy,
Death's cold arms will you embrace,
And fix your mortal resting place.

Cho.—

44.   C. M.
This Life is Like a Stream.

Our lives are like a flowing stream,
   Whose source we cannot find;
Our ending, too, cannot be seen,
   Wrapped up in God's design.

But when life's slender thread is broke,
   One little spark is gone,
The summons comes—the fatal stroke—
   And we must follow on.

We fall a lifeless chunk of clay,
   And lay beneath the ground,
Until the resurrection day.
   We'll wait the trumpet's sound.

'Tis here we have the budding hour,
   The next will be the rose,
The next will bring the full-blown flower,
   A life of sweet repose.

45.   C. M.
The Reaper.

The reaper with his glistening sword,
   Is mowing down the field;
The ripening fruit of our dear Lord,
   To his broad sword must yield.

He's clipping down the sons of men,
   Laying low the golden grain,
The reaper thrusts his sickle in,
   The sheaves he'll bind again.

He'll gather in the precious wares,
    The treasures of the Lord,
And separate the ugly tares,
    According to His word.

The reaper's work will soon be done,
    The word already given,
The winnowing of chaff begun,
    The wheat be saved in heaven.

We'll there surround God's righteous throne,
    When gathered safely in,
From His broad fields they all will come,
    Cleansed from all earthly sin.

They need not fear the glittering sword,
    Nor fear the gathering band,
For those prepared by our dear Lord,
    Should welcome His command.

46.   C. M.

The Apostle Paul.

The Apostle Paul of God was sent
    Into the Gentile world,
And preached the truth where'er he went,
    Christ's banner he unfurled.

In perils in the wilderness,
    In perils on the sea,
Was often bowed in weariness,
    From false brethren forced to flee.

In watchings and in painfulness,
    In hunger and in thirst,

And fastings, want and nakedness,
  Were often on him thrust.

In labors more abundantly,
  And in dark prisons laid,
With bloody stripes repeatedly,
  Till he was almost dead.

Received his forty stripes, save one,
  Five times from Jews alone,
Was beaten with a heavy rod,
  And once by them was stoned.

His mission was from day to day,
  When he was called abroad,
To turn the Gentiles from their way,
  And to the church of God.

He fought the Lord's good fight, to find
  A long and peaceful rest,
Beyond the restless shores of time,
  A crown of righteousness.

47.   7s.

Children of God.

O ye heavenly host, rejoice
God's elect and own free choice,
Shout, ye little flock, and praise,
Jesus loves you, Jesus saves.

CHORUS:

  Come and join His hosts below,
  Come, dear saint and sinner too;

Without money, come and buy
Wine and milk to satisfy.

Come and praise the Father's Son,
Pray His holy will be done,
He who saved us and who died,
By His blood we're justified.

Cho.—

He will guide us through the storm,
If we lean upon His arm;
If we trust in him for all,
We shall never faint nor fall.

Cho.—

He will save us every hour,
Through His kind and loving power,
O arise and come to Him,
Serve and adore your heavenly King.

Cho.—

Come and join the heavenly band,
In one solid phalanx stand,
Precious gifts to all are given,
Rich rewards for them in heaven.

Cho.—

Come, O come and follow Him,
Follow Christ, your Savior, King;
We are journeying to the skies,
Come, dear sinner, come, arise.

Cho.—

48.   C. M.

The Preacher.

I'm called to preach the gospel truth,
    Good news I'm bound to tell;
To preach glad tidings to the world,
    For my Immanuel.

I'll go through rain, or cold, or heat,
    And travel till I die;
No place to stop, there's no retreat,
    Although I often try.

My mission is to trembling souls,
    Who've wandered far away;
Prepare them for the gospel feast,
    And for the heavenly day.

My Master calls and I must go,
    Out in the open field,
To hunt for poor and thirsty souls,
    Who by free grace are sealed.

I'll tell them Jesus died for sins,
    And how He rose again,
That they might from all sin be cleansed,
    And washed from every stain.

I'll preach the gospel o'er the land,
    Good news I'm bound to tell,
How Jesus saves poor, fallen man,
    I'll preach Immanuel.

49.
Church Home.

O give me a home where the lilies grow,
Down in the valleys where the clear waters
    flow;
Among the green cedars, in fields of sweet pine,
O there let me live to the end of my time.

O give me a home where the lilies grow,
Where cold is forbidden, the ice and the snow,
The voice of the turtle is heard in the land,
The fig tree growing in its home on the sand.

O give me a home where the lilies grow,
In the land of feasting where the loved ones go,
The home of the dove in the cliffs of the rocks,
Feeding at nooday with the kids of the flocks.

O give me a home where the lilies grow,
'Midst the trees of frankincense, myrrh and
    aloe,
By fountains of water, in gardens of green,
Where fair sons and daughters of Israel are
    seen.

O give me a home where the lilies grow,
Among Zion's daughters and sons here below,
Until the day's dawn drives the shadows away,
My heart's desire is 'mong the fair ones to stay.

O give me a home where the lilies grow,
To dwell in the garden like the young hart
    and roe,

Where fair as the moon and as clear as the sun,
Is the dove in the garden, the undefiled one.

O give me a home in these gardens below,
Where the loved ones feed among the lilies
  that grow,
The palm tree and olive, and fruit of the pine,
Where the loved ones dwell, for the gardens
  are thine.

O give me a home where the lilies grow,
Where the robes are all washed as white as the
  snow;
I'd eat of the honey and drink of the wine,
O there let me live to the end of my time.

50.   C. M.
Prayer.

We bow, O God, before Thy throne,
  We pray Thou wilt forgive,
Almighty God, O righteous One,
  Let sinners look and live.

We bow, O Lord, before Thy throne,
  Our hearts all filled with prayer,
That Thy poor, erring, faulty ones,
  May trust in Thine own care.

We beg a home within Thy courts,
  We make this humble plea,
O grant us, Lord, a home at last,
  To all Thy glories see.

51. 8s. 7s.

Weary Not.

Weary not, poor, trembling children,
   Though the hour be dark and drear;
We shall soon all meet in heaven,
   For the night of death is near.

We see the sun so gently sinking,
   And the shades of night appear,
All our days gone by in weeping,
   Still we trust a Savior near.

Our trembling arms around us folding,
   While we're sinking down with pain,
Jesus Christ in glory telling,
   That we all shall live again.

Faith and hope around us clinging,
   When we breathe our latest breath,
He who loved us then revealing,
   Though our tongues be still in death.

Then weary not, poor, helpless children,
   For our God is one of love,
We are traveling in this kingdom
   To His blissful courts above.

Weary not, poor, mourning children,
   If the world should scoff and frown,
God is love and never changing,
   Grace and love will be your crown.

O weary not, poor, dying children,
   Soon the clouds will break away;

Then you'll rest with God in heaven,
　In the climes of endless day.

52.　　　　　　　　　　　　　　　P. M.
Fallen Man.

We are all in the bondage of sin,
　We are all in the same open field,
Our garments polluted in sin all are laid,
　In one bundle of guiltiness sealed.

Enthralled in these prisons of clay,
　Our faces all covered with shame,
Estranged from our Father and driven away,
　Unworthy His heavenly name.

Our lives, like the speed of the wind,
　No changing or stopping their course,
But onward and forward we all pass along,
　By the same great, omnipotent force.

In one moment we bid all farewell,
　And silently pass through death's door,
The storms of this life we shall no longer tell,
　When we cross to the evergreen shore.

53.　　　　　　　　　　　　　　　C. M.
We Must Wait.

We long to view the spirit world,
　Surround the glorious throne;
With millions, millions, there we'd join,
　Forever there we'd roam.

Eternity, unfathomed sea,
   Forever we'd explore;
Beyond the confines of this world
   We'd rest forever more.

Not here, oh! no, we would not stay,
   On this cold, forlorn shore;
To God in heaven we'll look, and pray
   For rest forever more.

We long to view the spirit world.
   That sinless, spotless clime,
With millions, millions, there we'd join,
   But we would wait our time.

54.   C. M

Ever the Same.

A thousand times we beg and sigh,
   A thousand times we mourn,
In sackcloth and in ashes lie,
   A poor and guilty worm.

Around and 'round on earth we go,
   A poisoned sinner still;
Unable of ourselves to keep,
   Or to perform God's will.

Yet still we go, and still we mourn,
   Each day is such the case;
'Tis not for us to stay nor stop,
   While we on earth remain.

A feeble bark of trembling clay,
   A stranger here we roam;

We wait and talk, and ask and pray,
    We long and sigh for home.

55.   C. M.

We Come.

We come, O Lord, we come, we come,
    With songs and hymns to sing;
We come, rejoicing, Lord, in Thee,
    Our God, our heavenly King.

Our lighted lamps shine soft and bright,
    We on our course pursue,
But not by our own strength or might
    Shall we go safely through.

We come, O Lord, we come to greet
    With songs and hymns to sing;
O let us join in anthems sweet,
    To praise our heavenly King.

56.   8s. 7s.

To Concord Association.

Go on, go on, dear brethren, go,
    While I am left at home;
The wind will bear your joys to me,
    The welcome news will come.

Go on, for all is well with you,
    Your joys and hopes are one,
You're sprinkled with the love of God,
    Your heavenly life begun.

Go on, dear brethren in the Lord,
    And may your joys o'erflow,

But I am left once more at home,
   With you I cannot go.

Go on, dear brethren, sing and pray,
   From house to house rejoice,
While I am left at home to stay—
   Methinks I hear your voice

Pour out your souls in earnest prayer,
   Your daily drink and meat;
The Lord will surely kindly hear,
   And you he'll surely keep.

O could I go with you today,
   'Twould be my heart's delight;
If I could go and with you stay,
   'Twould drive away the night.

Go on, dear brethren, fill your place,
   My mind will follow you,
Your journeyings my soul will trace,
   'Tis all that I can do.

Go on once more to old Concord,
   There feel the tie that binds,
While I am weak and faint at home,
   In sackcloth left behind.

57.   C. M.

We Would Skip the Hills.

We stand amazed, and wonder how
   Poor mortals on are borne;
O could we understand and know
   How Christ our souls adorns!

We'd see the lovely and the good,
  In every clime and place,
If we did know, or only could,
  That we are saved by grace.

But we draw back with fear and dread,
  And shake at death's approach,
And while it hovers round us near,
  We dread its awful touch.

Death's an angel with a roll
  And calling children home;
But how we sorrow when we're told
  That death's dark hour has come.

Beyond the crooked turns of life
  We pass beyond these scenes;
Oh! could we climb the distant heights,
  And skip the hills between.

58.   C. M.

To Die is Gain.

Why should we mourn or care to die
  When life is but a span?
Our days and weeks so swift go by,
  Them we can scarcely scan.

This life is like a raging gale
  That breaks upon our land,
With rains and winds and beating hail
  Which we can hardly stand.

'Tis but one cold and chilly blast
  In all the world around;

A wicked, wild and wayward race
    In every place is found.

O let us be prepared to die,
    Break off from every harm—
So many curses passing by
    In every shape and form.

O can we not on God rely,
    And make for brighter pearls?
O shall we not prepare to die
    And reach the spirit world?

59.   C. M.

The Conflict.

O give us strength and power, Lord,
    To conquer every foe;
For in our bosom dwells discord
    That leads to deepest woe.

Down in a dark and loathsome pit,
    Our minds so often plunge;
O if we only could but sit
    And see Thee our sins expunge.

O could we banish evil thought,
    Subdue the carnal will,
Drive out all notious satan's brought,
    With which our minds to fill.

We'd let our minds then soar aloft
    Into the heavenly field;
Our darkened lamps shine bright and soft,
    In light be reconciled.

60. C. M.

Sweet to Meet.

How sweet it is to dwell with God,
    And walk with Him below,
Be ever mindful of His word,
    And where He wishes go.

How sweet, how sweet, O Lord, how sweet,
    Here in the gospel land,
Where saints in loving friendship meet
    In one fraternal band.

How sweet, how sweet, O Lord, how sweet,
    To meet each other here;
In chambers of our God we meet
    With loving words of cheer.

How sweet, how sweet, O Lord, how sweet,
    While time goes rolling on,
In hope, and love, and faith to greet,
    Until life's day is gone.

61. C. M.

We Will Pass On.

Oh! what is life, or what is gain,
    If we could longer stay?
'Tis frought with troubles, toil and pain,
    And trials on the way.

Our suffering days and years roll on,
    They soon will all be o'er;
We're traveling fast, we're passing on
    Unto another shore.

The silent grave awaits our form,
    For it is only clay;
We live and die and so pass on,
    Unto another day.

O if God's spirit dwells within,
    If we are born again,
We'll rise with Christ and live with Him
    Beyond this world of pain.

62.
Each One Must Bear His Part.

Our hearts all pant for waters sweet,
    They crave the sweetest bread;
They crave the best to drink and eat,
    On whitest loaves to feed.

We go and come, and come and go,
    By tempests tossed about;
And to our journey's end must row,
    And soon we'll find it out.

The flower opens for the sun,
    It drinks the morning dew,
And to the breeze its fragrance sheds,
    Till torn and withered, too.

Though aches and pains, and sorrows, too,
    And troubles fill the heart,
When these all come—'tis nothing new—
    Each one must bear his part.

63.   8s. 6s.
Our Life.

Our life is full of faulty steps,
    But those we would disown,

Though can't prevent, for in they've crept,
    At every crook and turn.

We asked not for this life below,
    Where pain and sorrows come;
When fondest hopes are all aglow,
    Then death surrounds our home.

Life is a short, meandering stream,
    A crooked way at best;
Though along the little foot-path gleams,
    A cheering hope of rest.

Our brightest hopes lie just beyond
    The clouds that intervene;
We walk by faith, and not by sight—
    The lights are almost seen.

64.   8s. 6s.

Religion is Life and Light.

A lighted candle lights the house,
    Where all was dark within;
It shows the loathsome, filthy spots,
    Which had not else been seen.

The heart of man is cold and dark,
    'Till heaven's light reveals
The sin-deseased—the leprous spots—
    Which were before concealed.

Religion is the light of man,
    (The Spirit doth not sin;)
A work the spirit of God began,
    A blessed light within.

This life is pure and white as snow,
   When first it comes from God;
The Spirit like a snow-white dove,
   Takes up its sure abode.

It melts the cold and frozen heart—
   It thaws with love divine,
And tenders every stony part—
   I pray it touches mine.

65.   S. M.

My Works and Ways.

My works and ways are bad,
   My thoughts are so impure;
The many years that I have lived,
   All self-righteousness should cure.

With troubles, cares and tears,
   Along life's crooked stream,
So many trials, doubts and fears,
   Along where I have been.

I would not ask to live
   Another life of sin;
I could not bear the toil and pain.
   Of such a life again.

In all my lonely days,
   While journeying neath the sun,
I've longed to find some better ways
   Than my poor ways have been.

Should peace adorn the end,
   Or glory shine upon,

I could not for my works contend
  Or hang my hopes thereon.

O let the moments pass—
  Fly past till all are o'er;
For good or bad, I've come at last
  To death's dark chilly door.

66.   C. M.
        Entangled With the Enemy.

Out in a dark and dreary land,
  Poor, wretched sinners lay;
The iron monster crouched within;
  By him we're led astray.

Poor, careworn strangers strolling on,
  And crying mournfully,
Forwarned of God's great judgment morn,
  And of eternity.

O what amazing sight to see
  The children of our God,
Estranged from him, and from him flee,
  And disobey his word.

How precious is their time below,
  For death is drawing near;
How precious are the hours that go,
  For God's dear children here.

67.   8s. 7s.
            My Poor Life.

My poor life is almost ended,
  I am tired, weak and worn,

Long and dreary days I've wended,
   Many sorrows I have borne;
Full of tears and full of crosses,
   From all of which I cannot flee,
But I will not ask the causes,
   They will soon all pass from me.

Now I'd love to be accepted,
   Though I cannot change the past:
With my works and ways rejected,
   I must trust in Christ at last;
When at first this life beginning,
   A young and tender, careless boy,
Satan's leagues so kind and winning,
   Planned my whole life to destroy.

Now my feeble life is waning,
   I feel I'm traveling in the night;
But a beacon light is burning,
   Across the thorny steps in sight;
O this world is a world of danger,
   Danger all along the line;
While I'm traveling as a stranger,
   Could I but improve my time?

Only just a few steps farther—
   And I'm stumbling still along—
I will then unload forever,
   All my burdens will be gone;
Once across the dangerous ocean,
   Then I'd dearly love to tell,
Of my lot and peaceful portion,
   In the Lord I hope to dwell.

At the hour of my departing,
  Could I speak a word of cheer,
To my friends who are left behind me—
  Tell them of a Savior dear;
Now the night of death is nearing,
  And the lonely grave appears,
We hear the voices of angels telling,
  Dry up all your lonely tears.

68. P. M.
The Gospel Bell.

O the gospel bell is ringing
  Clear and loud o'er this land,
And sinners they are falling,
  By His power, the great I Am;
O the gospel bell is ringing,
  Run up the banner high,
The under shepherd's telling
  Of the sweet by and by.

O the gospel bell is ringing,
  The army's on the road,
Valiant soldiers, they are fighting
  For the kingdom of our God;
O the gospel bell is ringing,
  O why not join our band?
The road is smooth and easy
  Here in this gospel land.

O the gospel bell is ringing,
  The war is on to stay;
The battle cry of freedom
  Sounds along the gospel way;

O the gospel bell is ringing,
  The sound is loud and long;
Gallant soldiers are now shouting,
  King Jesus is their song.

O the gospel bell is ringing,
  Run up the banner high,
The war cry is for victory,
  And we'll fight until we die;
O the gospel bell is ringing,
  Run up the banner high;
The under shepherd's telling
  Of the sweet by and by.

69.   8s. 7s.
Thankfulness.
When the earth is filled with fulness,
  'Tis for each and every soul,
All their hearts o'errun with gladness,
  They cannot their joys control;
The great harvest yields its sweetness,
  Most delicious food for man,
Loaded down with richest substance,
  Over all the earth's fair land.

Rocked in riches from the cradle.
  Thousands rest in calm repose,
Have no fears, and dread no evil,
  So the world in fatness goes;
Millions care not for each other,
  While they drink the cup of gain,
For one's self and not for brother,
  So they love to live and reign.

Our God showers down great blessings,
    The early and the later rain,
Brings the fruitful crops in season,
    Shout his praise with glad acclaim!
He bestows with great abundance,
    'Tis through him man hopes to live;
Yet unmindful of his givings,
    So unthankful he receives.

When unthankful for his givings,
    "He's ungrateful that receives,"
Doth not, with his heart-felt kindness,
    Love His good and tender ways;
Many men from Him do wander,
    With their minds so far away;
While God clothes them in such grandeur,
    They should be thankful every day.

It is God that clothes and feeds them,
    With his blessings from above,
And they should all try to please him,
    With their daily thanks and love,
Ever mindful of his goodness,
    Ever more should praise his name;
Never will the Lord forget us,
    If we'll humbly follow him.

71.   C. M.
God Does All.

O what am I but dust and clay?
    A weak and broken reed,

A fallen nature to obey,
    A sinful worm indeed!

I cannot pay one farthing's worth
    With my own righteousness;
My works, my words, my deeds and thoughts,
    With God are valueless.

I was a sinner, God doth know,
    And all was dark within,
The carnal mind my bitterest foe,
    My daily drink was sin.

I found at last a mournful cry,
    And mercy was my theme;
Appeal to God at once or die,
    I could only look to him.

The precious hour, the time had come,
    My aching heart relieved,
And not a farthing's worth I'd done,
    I could not God deceive.

That which I loved I now forsake,
    My lot of sin and shame,
The great broad way I now did hate,
    The way in which I came.

God draws the sinner by His grace
    From a drear wilderness;
'Tis his great love poor sinners taste,
    And his own righteousness.

'Twas God who taught my soul within,
    'Twas God that made me cry,

'Twas God who pardoned all my sin
And me prepared to die.

72.   L. M.

O Could I Tell.

O could I, with my stammering tongue,
Find words to praise the Father's Son;
O could I raise my voice on high,
I'd sound his praise up to the sky.

O could I lisp some words of praise,
To tell of my Redeemer's ways,
I'd tell of Christ, our faithful friend,
And praise His name unto the end.

O could I find some words to tell
Glad tidings of Immanuel!
O could I praise His glorious name,
And with my tongue aloud proclaim.

O could I tell of God's dear Son,
And of the holy, righteous one;
O could I tell of his free grace,
His wondrous love and righteousness.

73.   L. M.

The Good Old Way.

Children are fed in pastures green,
From time to time, with food unseen,
By Parent dear, from day to day,
When walking in the good old way.

But some are in the cold, bare field,
The watchman calls, they will not yield,
And drooping on from day to day,
They ask not for the good old way.

While others hear the tender voice,
And come and feast where food is choice;
Their Master's word they do obey,
And walk along the good old way.

But some among the wild beasts roam,
Away from friends, away from home;
They care not for the call, they say,
And leave the path—the good old way.

And drifting on with bleak winds cold,
The warning words of them are told—
The trumpet sounding, day by day,
To seek the paths—the good old way.

Do hearken to the watchman's call,
Renounce the world and give up all,
And come and feed here day by day,
Along the paths—the good old way.

The old lie out to starve and die,
And the tender lambs, who beg and cry,
Are holding back from day to day,
And ask not for the good old way.

Oh! children dear, out in the storm,
Do, pray come home, away from harm;
You are invited day by day,
To Zion's path—the good old way.

Good, rich, ripe food, the purest kind,
So gently given, so well refined;
How can you now refuse to stay,
Outside the paths—the good old way?

A full supply always on hand,
Direct from heaven, the promised land;
Oh! why not come, just now obey,
Walk in the paths—the good old way.

74.   C. M.
Angels.

O let the holy angels come,
  The immortal hosts of heaven,
And bring glad tidings from our home—
  The home by God's grace given.

O come, O come, sweet angels, come,
  And bring the gladsome news,
Your cheering words and friendly touch,
  How could we dare refuse?

O come and cheer us on our way,
  Poor prisoners bound in sin,
With iron fetters day by day,
  And heavy hearts within.

We're traveling o'er the mountain paths,
  And across the dangerous streams,
All bruised and bleeding on our way;
  Such dreadful, frightful scenes!

We would not long on earth remain,
  We'd leave this sinful clime;

O if we could with you ascend,
    And heavenly mansions find!

O we will wait your kind return,
    Wait for the heavenly day,
Our festering bands that now are borne
    Will then be cut away.

Then we can fly to heaven with you,
    The angel lauds above,
We'll skip the gulf and mountains, too,
    And dwell with you in love.

75.   S. M.

Flying Hours.

The sun is sinking low
    Behind the distant hill;
The days and nights, how fast they go!
    They're never standing still.

Another day is gone,
    The lonely night appears;
How fast the hours go flying on!
    How fast the fleeting years!

We stretch out on our bed,
    Again we'll try to rest;
The flying hours are quickly sped,
    How soon the night is past!

We rise at morning dawn,
    But on and on they fly;
They're rushing on with every sun,
    And so are you and I.

76. 7s.

Shall We Hope to Live Again?

Is this mortal life a dream?
Birth, and life, and death-bed scene?
Shall we hope to live again?
Shall our hopes be all in vain?

Fresh from the cradle, as of old,
Wrestling with the world for gold,
Early man begins to fight;
Wealth and fame are his delight.

Nature's children, what are we?
After death where shall we be?
Infants are born, and live and die;
Who can tell the causes why?

Shall we look and hope in vain
For a life to live again?
Who can tell or who can know
Why we come or this way go?

Short the life of man, indeed,
Flying through with lightning speed,
Tossed about with worldly care,
Yet his landing draweth near.

Morning's light and evening's sun,
Then our course is almost run;
Evening shades and fading light,
Quickly followed by the night.

When life's brittle thread is broke,
And we've thrown off this mortal yoke,

When we feel death's biting sting,
May we hope to live again?

Yes, we hope to live again,
Live a life made free from pain;
Of that life God only knows,
Where man dwells, or where he goes.

When we think of what we are,
Then we're filled with dark despair;
With a sorrow, tear and sigh,
Grieved because we're born to die.

We cannot change our mortal course,
Carried on by such great force;
Every thing there is in sight,
Travels on with day and night.

Yet we trust that some great power
Doth control and rule the hour;
Subject to that power we stand—
All is ruled by its strong hand.

We will look, and watch, and wait,
We will trust the unseen Great;
What we do, for that we're slain,
Yet we hope to live again.

When our earthly course is run,
When the thread of life is spun,
With the last expiring breath,
Heaven's light may shine in death.

Fading world of sin and pain!
Yes, we hope to live again;

Before the judge of heaven's land,
There for good or bad we'll stand.

Far beyond the gloom of night,
All the mist cleared up and bright;
Endless joy may be our lot,
This dark page of life forgot.

77.   C. M.

The Lord Knows Our Way.

The Lord our God doth surely know
   How in this flesh we dwell;
How thorny is the road we go,
   The Lord doth know full well.

Here in this feeble, human frame,
   We're tempest tossed and bound;
So full of cares and full of pain,
   Here in this dungeon found.

'Tis not for us to stay or stop,
   Long in this mortal prison;
And many tears of anguish drop,
   From our poor souls are riven.

On life's cold stream we float along,
   And fate seems hovering near;
How oft our boat seems dashed aground,
   When dangerous waves appear.

We long and pine for distant hills,
   We'd scale the mountains high,
For some green spot our souls to fill,
   For this we groan and sigh.

We from the cup of sin do drink,
   Our natural thirst to assuage,
But our poor souls, so weak and faint,
   Crave sweeter beverage.

We dream of purer, brighter lands,
   For angel lands we sigh,
Beyond the beating storms of time,
   We hope, for you and I.

78.   C. M.

The Triune God.

The Father, Holy Ghost and Word
   Abide with sinful man;
The workings of the triune God
   Make known the righteous plan.

The Father, Holy Ghost and word,
   Compose the three in one;
And the Spirit, water and the blood,
   Also agree in one.

The witness of the living God,
   The Spirit testified,
Of the great work which he had done
   When Christ was crucified.

Our Lord doth give eternal life;
   This life is in His Son;
He spilt His blood, and when He died,
   The mighty work was done.

79.   C. M.
The Time To Die.

When I was young I sought the road,
   Of which wealth is the test;
But now I'm old, I crave not gold,
   I crave a sweeter rest.

I love the earth all clothed in green;
   I do not wish to die,
Till cold December's chills have come,
   O then my soul would fly.

I love the earth when it is seen
   Beneath the warm, blue sky—
The hills, and trees, and mountains green,
   O then I would not die.

The cheerful spring returns, you know,
   Drives back the winter's gloom;
The trees grow green and meadows, too,
Send forth their rich perfume.

I love the gladsome, spring-like days,
   The happiest of the year;
But like the days of my boyhood,
   They quickly disappear.

I love the woods adorned in green,
   But soon the leaves will fall;
Then I'd sleep 'neath the moon's pale beam,
   And gladly give up all.

The time, or how, we're not to choose,
   When from this world we part;

We'll make no choice, no time refuse,
   That falls to our sad lot.

The solemn, melancholy call
   Of death we soon shall hear;
The time allotted here for all
   Is daily drawing near.

80.   C. M.
Death's Unbroken Chain.

The chains of death around us wound
   Are festering links that bind,
And children of the flesh are found
   In great distress of mind.

We have no power to break the chains
   And gain our liberty;
Grim monster, death, forever reigns,
   From it we cannot flee.

Death's beating billows round us roll
   With every changing wind;
The current strong we now behold
   Down on our flesh descend.

Why should we mourn, lament and cry,
   At death's unbroken chain?
For grace will melt it all away
   And free us from its pain.

81.   C. M.
Gloom O'ershadows the Mind.

O I'm a poor, lost sinner, Lord,
   Thy law I cannot fill;

Unable of myself to keep,
  Or to perform Thy will.

O could I walk with humble feet,
  The open pathway made,
Thy footsteps and Thy track I'd keep,
  And do as Thou hast said.

How can I claim the Lord my own,
  And go so far astray?
Shall I be banished from His throne,
  And from the eternal day.

82.   C. M.
Pain and Sorrow.

From pain and sorrow let us pass,
  From all our worldly cares,
The sufferings of our mortal flesh,
  The anguish and the tears.

Borne down in sorrow and in pain,
  Our life is but a dream;
What gloomy thoughts pervade the mind,
  Such little light can gleam.

O our decaying forms must die,
  Return unto the ground;
O how we mourn, lament and cry;
  No other way is found.

83.   C. M.
A Poor, Lone Beggar.

O I'm a poor, lone beggar, Lord,
  A sinning man of dust;

A poor, lone beggar at Thy feet,
    I am poor and weak at best.

O I'm a poor and guilty worm,
    A crawling worm of clay;
Worthless and helpless, Lord, I mourn,
    Along the lonesome way.

We ask, O God, for mercies great,
    For favors not a few;
For we are tired, poor and weak,
    And know not what to do.

84.   C. M.

God's People.

O had I power to reconcile
    God's people here below,
I'd raise my voice and loud I'd cry,
    Wherever I do go.

I'd gladly comfort and console,
    Along the uneven way;
I'd bear their troubles and their load,
    On each and every day.

For them my heart within me moves,
    For them I try to pray,
For them my soul within is stirred,
    With them I'll ever stay.

Oh! could I meet them all below,
    And tell of Jesus' worth,
To them I'd fly, yea, gladly go,
    Be reconciled in death.

85. P. M.
Follow Him.

When the sun refused to shine on Golgotha's
    rugged brow,
  Where the Savior of sinners was slain;
'Twas there he bore their sins, and for them
    his head did bow;
  All hail! blessed One, follow Him.

CHORUS:

Follow Him, follow Him, all hail! blessed One,
    follow Him;
  In the blood of the Lamb,
  In the blood of the Son,
All hail! blessed One, follow Him.

Let us taste of the goodness that flows from
    his blood,
  And bear with our suffering and pain;
Let us drink from the fountain of His redeem-
    ing love;
  All hail! blessed One, follow Him.

CHO.—

We will follow the path that our Savior has trod,
  And we'll suffer the grief and the shame;
We will follow the meek and the lowly Son of
    God;
  All hail! blessed One, follow him.

CHO.—

Let us drink of the cup and we'll eat of His
    bread,
  And forever will praise him and sing;

We will take up our cross and will humbly be led,
All hail! blessed One, follow Him.

Cho.—

When at last we shall soar to that home upon high,
And when our poor bodies are changed,
We will sing, hallelujah, with wings we shall fly;
All hail! blessed One, follow Him.

Cho.—

86.   C. M.

The Church.

How firm and solid is the rock,
   On which the church is built;
And Christ is the builder and support,
   For it His blood was spilt.

Christ is the sure foundation stone,
   Upon which the building stands,
The framework all by Him alone,
   Was wrought by His own hand.

The winds, and storms, and floods may beat,
   Upon this building hard,
But it will stand in Him complete,
   For Christ was daily guard.

Kept as the apple of His eye,
   The glory of His cause,
He lingers always round it nigh—
   By grace his people draws.

'Tis like the bright and morning star,
  Out in the clear blue sky,
The church illuminates afar,
  And God doth glorify.

Firm as the rock his people stand,
  The glory of the Lord,
Upheld and fed by his own hand,
  And by the gospel word.

87.   S. M.
A Prayer.

O friends, why should we mourn?
  Or why these doubts and fears?
If God shines in our souls
  He'll sweeten all our tears.

O let the curtain rise,
  Between us and our God;
May he open all our eyes
  That we may see the road.

Then would our burdened souls
  Break forth in strains of joy,
That sin's dark spots and stains
  No more our peace destroy.

88.   P. M.
Thankfulness.

O how thankful we are,
  When God's favors appear,
When the ground is all parched up and dry;

O how thankful are we,
When his favors we see,
Handed down from the uppermost sky.

We are helpless, indeed,
We are poor and in need,
All are standing at mercy's kind door;
But we are thankful again,
When the Lord sends us rain,
All his children are thankful once more.

O we fall at His feet.
Taste of mercies so sweet,
Flowing from the fair lands up above;
O we beg and implore,
And we'll praise and adore
Our great King for his mercy and love.

O let's praise Him and sing,
Our dear Savior and King,
Let's remember the Lord up on high:
O how thankful are we,
When his blessings we see,
Handed down from the uppermost sky.

89. L. M.
In the Woods Alone.

Beneath the sun's bright shining rays
I love to dwell and spend my days;
I love to sing, and talk, and pray,
And tell of Jesus on the way.

I love to view the landscape o'er;
I love to walk along the shore;
From hill to hill, from sea to sea,
O could I roam and tell of thee!

The winds so softly fan my face,
While traveling on from place to place;
In every plant, and leaf, and flower,
God's grace and love shines every hour.

No tongue can tell nor pen portray
The beauty of one summer day;
O what a grand and winning sight!
The woods and hills are my delight.

O when this mortal life shall cease,
When I shall quit this lovely place,
O will this world with shining love
Outdo the mansions high above?

O no, these hills will not compare,
With heaven's mansions high, up there;
Unfading beauties far surpass—
Their splendor will forever last.

O may we reach the heavenly hill,
And find its joy our hearts to fill,
Rejoice and praise the heavenly day,
In pleasant fields that ne'er decay.

90.   C. M.
We Must Look Beyond.

O child of God, what have we found
In this cold world below,

But clouds, and storms, and perils, too,
  Wherever we do go?

O what is life but dread and fear,
  Affliction's heavy chain?
We cannot help the falling tear
  While we on earth remain.

We'll pass beyond the heavy rod,
  We'll step beyond its stroke,
We'll fly away and be with God,
  The final end of hope.

91.   C. M.
Remember Ye the Lord.

The Lord is always good and kind,
  Remember ye the Lord;
And we shall always blessings find
  In the keeping of His word.

Our life is but a single span,
  Its just one rolling wave
At every step, and crook and turn,
  We're hastening to the grave.

We should remember God, indeed,
  For He is good and kind,
If we would be by Him received,
  And heaven's glories find.

92.
They Are Gathering Home.

Our Savior dwells in brighter lands,
His children come when He commands;

Our dying day is drawing near.
Before King Jesus we'll appear.

CHORUS:

They're gathering home, they're gathering home;
The nations all are gathering home.

From forest, field and landscape o'er,
From distant lands, on every shore,
From all the hills and flowery plains,
They're gathering home where Jesus reigns.

CHO—

The seas may roar and billows break,
The earth may tremble, reel and shake,
Yet God is gathering one by one,
From every land, from every tongue.

CHO.—

The world may gaze and stand amazed,
With millions, millions half way crazed,
Still He is gathering, one by one,
His faithful and His chosen ones.

CHO.—

O, children dear, believe his word,
If you should cry you would be heard;
O turn, repenting sinner, turn,
For God will spare you and not burn.

CHO.—

While God is calling, thousands come
From every quarter, still there's room;

They're gathering home, they're gathering home,
From every land beneath the sun.

Cho.—

93. C. M.

Song.

Behold, the clouds are hanging low,
    The distant thunders roar,
The ceaseless winds continuous blow.
    O'er all this lonesome shore.

Our drooping, changing, shifting minds.
    Are clouded like the day;
Our home-tried friends, so good and kind,
    In death are called away.

We'll leave the earth, with all its load
    Of misery, want and crime;
We're swiftly moving on to God.
    This world we'll leave behind.

94. C. M.

Armies of the Living God.

O let the sparkling camp fires burn,
    As in the days of yore;
Ten thousand thousand hearts still yearn
    For Canaan's happy shore.

The armies of the living God.
    With banners waving high,

Move on towards the happy land—
    And who can them defy?

Away, away, O let them fly,
    True soldiers of the Lord;
The fruitful hills are towering high
    Beyond the swelling flood.

With camp outfits and tents they move,
    And shoes that never wear,
With heavenly manna from above,
    And none shall lack a share.

O let the living armies move,
    As in the days of yore;
Ten thousand, thousand, hearts of love,
    For Canaan's happy shore.

95.   C. M.
Unregenerated.

We cannot change the hearts of men,
    Nor take their sins away,
Nor make their bosoms swell with love,
    To ask for endless day.

The dark, the cold, the unborn soul,
    In folly loves to bask,
To live again or be made whole—
    He willeth not to ask.

The lifeless world is speeding on,
    Almost with lightning speed;
This craving world is hurled along,
    Its life is crime and greed.

96. C. M.
God Gives the Life.

We cannot tell, we do not know,
    Just why we are sure to die,
Unless it be for what we do—
    Perhaps this may be why.

We're fallen creatures at our best,
    God did not make us so;
But we're all lost in mortal flesh,
    And on to ruin we go.

For we were poisoned in the fall—
    The sting of death is sin;
We're lost and helpless, one and all,
    Unless we're saved by Him.

God does not now design to give,
    For what we claim or say;
Our natures could not be received,
    For this is not His way.

He is holy, perfect, pure and clean,
    While we are only flesh;
We could not be received by Him,
    Till we are made afresh.

God clothes the tree in living green,
    It could not clothe itself;
He gives to us the life unseen,
    With inward righteousness.

97. C. M.
Return, Repent.

Repent, repent, O man, repent,
 Return unto the Lord;
To you the great salvation's sent,
 Repent, obey the word.

Repent, repent, O man, repent,
 And turn from every sin;
Look to the Lord and be ye saved,
 O turn and look to him.

Repent, O son of man, repent,
 The law you have within;
Why will you not obey the Lord?
 O turn and look to Him.

Thou feeble son of man, repent,
 Good works just now begin;
Deny yourself and look to Christ,
 O turn and look to Him.

He is your bright and morning star—
 O can't you follow Him?
The Spirit and the bride say come,
 O turn from every sin.

Repent, repent, O man, repent,
 Look to the Lord and live;
To you His great salvation's sent,
 O turn, and He'll forgive.

98. L. M.
Friendly Home to Come.

There's only a few that I have found,
That seem to be like me, cast down;
Or realize their dreadful state,
Or call on God for mercies great.

I could not ask, or mourn, or pray,
Till Jesus led me in the way;
How could I rightly call on Him,
Till I was shown my guilt and sin?

O what is life with all its pain,
If we're not blessed and born again?
And if there's not some brighter home
Beyond this sin-stained world to come?

Distresses thick around me lie—
O who will answer when I cry,
If there's no power that will us save,
Or raise our bodies from the grave?

O dark and lonely is my way,
With anxious thoughts each day by day;
And my poor mind is so distressed—
This is my lot, I must confess.

God gives the life and takes away,
And we have not one word to say;
We suffer pain, pass on and die,
But dare not ask the causes why.

O gladly would we reach the end,
If God would only mercies send;

L of C.

If he will hear us when we cry,
   Then we'll be reconciled to die.

O, let the hours and moments fly
   If God will meet us at the last—
Unveil the hidden life to come,
   And greet us with a friendly home.

99.   C. M.
Sing Songs in Praise to God.

O for a sweeter song to sing
   The praises of our God;
Much fresher, sweeter anthems bring,
   To sound His praise abroad.

Go, sing, and tell the glorious news,
   Salvation, oh! how sweet;
For both the Gentiles and the Jews,
   Salvation's made complete.

O sing a sweeter, nobler song,
   Our tongues to lisp His praise;
O let our psalms and hymns prolong,
   Make known His righteous ways.

100.   L. M.
The Bitter Cup.

O can I not refuse to taste,
And take my flight and onward haste?
O can I not refuse the cup?
Or from its contents must I sup?

O my poor soul from it doth shrink
And of its contents would not drink;

But when its dying groans are heard
Its bitter then may not be feared.

O could I sup without a sigh,
Taste of the cup and drink it dry,
Then I might view the greater throng,
March through the gates with joyful song.

The light, the joy, that love-lit place
Reflecting from our Father's face,
Will compensate for all our tears—
Then God will drive away all fears.

101.   C. M.
The Church.

Can heaven be more beauteous, Lord,
    Than Zion's fields below,
When peace abounds, and no discord
    Disturbs love's joyous flow?

We walk around the garden walls,
    Inside the lovely gates;
The fig tree putteth forth green figs,
    The vine its tender grapes.

Along the garden paths we stroll,
    And view the heavenly land;
The growing plants before our eyes
    In blushing beauty stand.

How happy is the man of God
    Inside the heavenly wall;
While strolling along the garden walks
    How can he ever fall?

102.   C. M.

Our Delight.

(MAY 18, 1897.)

We love to sit beneath the trees,
  On warm and sunny days,
Where none molest, or make afraid,
  While we our Savior praise.

We love to live in peace, and speak
  Of our Redeemer's name;
How good and excellent His ways,
  Aloud we would proclaim.

We love the woods, the hills, and streams,
  And all that God has made;
We love to glorify His name,
  Out in the lovely shade.

And when the world is lost to sight,
  Our mind goes flying on;
God's grace still holds us in the light,
  While we are traveling home.

103.   C. M.

Our Joys.

Among the little social bands
  My fondest joys they lie;
Where God's refulgent glory shines
  To all the passers by.

We cross the rocks and fords below,
  We journey o'er the hills,

And onward to Mount Zion go,
  Our thirsting souls to fill.

Refresh our souls with love divine,
  God's glorious gift to man;
It guides us through the wilderness,
  On to the heavenly land.

O may it dwell within our breast.
  And linger round us nigh;
Its light may shine around us bright,
  To all the passers by.

104.
Grace Paid it All.

I have traveled the ocean stream,
  Its wealth was my aim;
I found only vision's dream
  Of luster and fame;
All, all was dark and cold,
Without grace to warm the soul;
All, all was strife within,
  This world to gain.

I have sought all the joys of life,
  While wandering around,
But I gained only grief and strife,
  Few pleasures I found;
Earth's troubles filled my breast,
Till my soul it could not rest.
Great streams of anguish flow.
  Here, here below.

O I mingled with joy and mirth,
  But all, all was vain;
I sought for the wealth of earth,
  And it tried to gain;
Soon, then, I made complaint,
For my flesh was weak and faint,
Trembling I sought relief,
  All, all in tears.

O I labored incessantly,
  But all brought no peace;
And as I suffered distressingly,
  'Twas then I found grace
The Lord bestowed on me;
Jesus found and set me free,
Grace all my days shall see,
  Grace paid it all.

Grace found me in my sins,
  'Twas grace all the way;
It was grace shined my soul within,
  And taught me to pray;
Grace, grace shall be my song,
Grace that led my soul along,
Grace, grace shall be my theme,
  Grace paid it all.

105   L. M.

The Gospel Plan.

There are many ways devised by man,
But God prepared the gospel plan;

Ordained it to save sinners, poor,
And grace and power make it sure.

Ye fearful, trembling, weeping souls,
The gospel plan will make you whole
O watch, poor sinners, hear the cry,
The gospel day is passing by.

Be not encumbered with much care,
Nor drift along in dark despair;
But prune your worldly natures down,
And sit beneath the gospel sound.

Our time is short, we all must die,
O will you not to Jesus fly,
And with your Savior spend your days?
Subdue your cold and formal ways,

Then we can praise the King of heaven,
And rest content with favors given;
Obey the glorious gospel plan,
Prepared to save rebellious man.

106. C. M.
Gospel Tidings.

Arise, ye nations, arise and hear
  The glorious gospel sound;
Proclaim glad tidings far and near,
  To all the world around.

O spread abroad the glorious news,
  The gospel jubilee;
Among the Gentiles and the Jews,
  Proclaim, Salvation's free.

The glorious gospel news go tell,
  The trumpet's joyful sound,
The sweet vibrating echo's swell
  To earth's remotest bound.

Prepare a table, spread a feast,
  Invite all nations in;
The wise, the tall, the great, and least,
  To sup with Christ their King.

Ring, O ring the gospel bell,
  Let all the nations know;
Glad tidings of salvation tell,
  To all the world below.

O blow the trumpet, sound the call,
  For all the royal guests;
Invite the nations, great and small,
  To come to Christ and rest.

107.
Wandering Pilgrim.

I'm a poor, old, wandering pilgrim,
  Ofttimes resting in the shade;
Many days and nights been traveling
  On my earthly pilgrimage;
I've been resting by the roadside,
  'Neath the shade trees along the way,
In my lonely hours been thinking
  Of the long, eternal day.

Over hill, and vale, and mountain,
  With my stay and staff in hand,

Along the rough, uneven journey,
    In a poor, sin-stricken land;
There are no beds made soft and downy,
    No soft pillows for my head,
And the way is rough and thorny—
    I ofttimes wish that I was dead.

I'm a poor, old, wandering pilgrim,
    Heavy laden on the way,
Great and many are my afflictions,
    Growing greater every day;
I will ask the Lord to help me,
    And hold up my feeble hands,
And to take me in His bosom,
    And to take me as I am.

When at last my journey's ended,
    I hope to reach that radiant shore,
In the long and glad forever,
    Where sin and troubles are no more;
It's a resting place for strangers,
    Who are traveling on the way;
It's a resting place for pilgrims,
    Land of rest! O longed-for day.

108.
In Peace.

Once more we're all in peace,
    Once more our hearts unite,
And every act, and word, and thought,
    Express our soul's delight.

O let us then rejoice,
   In one fraternal band.
All in one union, with one voice,
   All joined in heart and hand.

Let every tongue proclaim
   Aloud the tie that binds;
Each throbbing heart declare the same,
   The love and peace it finds.

In mutual love and peace,
   The Lord doth surely bless;
The smiling of each loving face,
   Bespeaks true happiness.

Go on and serve the Lord,
   Each one his place to fill;
We'll all go on without discord,
   To do our Master's will.

109.
The Good Old Church.

Blest be the tie that binds
   Us to the old church home;
The same old spot we love to find,
   Where saints delight to come.

The good, old-fashioned house,
   Where Zion's children meet;
Beneath its worn and shattered roof,
   We oft our brethren greet.

We love the good old church,
   With all its tender ways;

We love to mingle with the saints,
   Join in their songs of praise.

How often there we've trod
   Upon the sacred ground,
Joined in the worship of our God,
   Where love and peace abound.

O how we love to find
   Our brethren all in peace;
The same old kindred tie that binds
   All to the dear old place.

Lo, many years have passed
   That we have served the Lord,
And in the same old-fashioned place,
   He feeds us on His word.

Our heads have now grown white,
   We'll soon turn pale and die,
We soon shall pass the stormy night,
   Reach dearer homes on high.

110.   C. M.
Be Ye Reconciled.

O, man of God, shed not a tear,
   Our trials will soon be o'er;
We'll leave this world, with all its care,
   For Canaan's happy shore.

O, man of God, why should you cry?
   The tears go streaming down!
We soon shall with the angels fly
   And rest with them at home.

O, man of God, why will you cry?
    O wipe your tears away;
There's peace and rest in yonder sky,
    A brighter, clearer day.

O, man of God, why would you stay,
    Long on this troubled shore?
From persecutions fly away,
    Where troubles are no more.

O, man of God, what shall we say
    To reconcile the mind?
We'll launch from these cold shores away
    And endless glory find.

O, man of God, look far away,
    Rejoice and sing aloud,
There's rest and peace from all the storms,
    Beyond the lowering cloud.

O, man of God, why will you cry,
    Or shake when death appears?
Its swinging gate will bring us joy;
    O dry your falling tears.

O, man of God, what shall we say?
    Our day will soon be o'er;
We soon shall quit this house of clay
    For Canaan's happy shore.

111.   C. M.

Desire for Baptism.

O how we longed to be baptized
    When first we knew the Lord!

And by the water lingered oft,
    Resolved to keep his word.

We'd follow him and keep the pledge,
    We'd do the Master's will;
We gathered round the water's edge,
    Obeyed His mandate still.

Buried with Christ into His death,
    In form as He had led,
We rose to walk in a new life
    And do as He had said.

The answer of a conscience good,
    Is the reward we earn ;
That brighter pathways we may find,
    And better precepts learn.

112.   8s. 6.

The Least.

O I'm the least of all the saints,
    If I am one at all ;
I'm troubled with the worst complaints,
    The worst that could befall.

"Tis sin and folly, grief and woe,
    That doth my soul annoy ;
The tempter comes—my bit'rest foe,
    And would my hope destroy.

113.   8s. 6.

Went Astray.

I know not, and I could not tell,
    When first I went astray ;

But from my sinful lips words fell,
   Throughout the live-long day.

O, dearest Lord, could I recall
   The words, the deeds, the crime,
The lot, the portion, and the all,
   Brought by the carnal mind.

'Tis our own faults that drag us down,
   They never build us up,
They leave us prone upon the ground,
   Without a single prop.

We fold our arms and think it good,
   We call the bitter, sweet,
The unclean nature always would
   The gall and wormwood eat.

We roll the morsel 'neath the tongue,
   We call it rich and rare,
The old-time song so often sung—
   "Let each one get his share."

Man's nature leads him to disown
   The God he should obey;
But all his wayward life was known,
   Before he went astray.

114.   C. M.

Cheer Up.

Cheer up, ye feeble, fainting souls,
   Dread not the bitter cup,
For Jesus claims you for his own,
   And He will raise you up.

Cheer up, ye feeble, fainting souls,
    For you Lord Jesus died;
His blood was spilt, it made you whole,
    When he was crucified.

Cheer up, ye feeble, fainting souls,
    No longer hide your face,
For Christ will take you safely home,
    Poor children, saved by grace.

Cheer up, ye feeble, fainting souls,
    Pray do not worship toys,
Beyond the glittering things of earth,
    You'll reap eternal joys.

115.   C. M.
A Debt of Gratitude to God.

O what a puny stick of clay,
    As worthless as a weed,
The law I never could obey,
    My heart's so filled with greed.

I could not pray, I could not cry,
    My heart was hard as steel,
I could not ask, I know not why,
    No evil conscience feel.

I did not realize my state,
    The guilty man of sin,
I did not see the sin to hate,
    Nor feel the guilt within.

But O, a pang of sorrow came,
    And quickly struck me down,

Gave me a bleeding heart, all torn,
    A stinging deadly wound.

Poor, puny stick of clay and dust,
    At last did now give way,
And to the Righteous and the Just,
    At once began to pray.

With sorrowing heart I called on God
    To come to my relief;
I felt that I had done no good,
    My sins, they brought me grief.

But grace and mercy manifest,
    While I was sore distressed,
Did raise me up, and O how blest!
    His love within I felt.

O Lord, our God, we trust in Thee,
    We feel Thy quickening power,
Thy grace alone hath made us free,
    We love Thee every hour.

116.   **C. M.**

Our Hope.

O Lord, we praise and chant thy name,
    We long to see thy face;
A crown of glory let us claim,
    And now we claim Thy grace.

Where everlasting springs abide,
    And rocks that never shake,
O, may Thy Spirit onward guide,
    And never us forsake.

O, come and wipe away all tears,
    All spots of sin and shame,
And let this blighted world of ours
    Get rid of every stain.

O, come and heal our every wound,
    Make glad our souls in peace,
Then let our hearts in love be found,
    Enlightened by Thy Grace.

117.   8s. 6.
The Gospel.

The glorious gospel's soothing sound
    Awakes the child of sin;
Poor, mourning children it hath found,
    And gently led them in.

At first it sounds much like a knell,
    And they are made to feel
Like standing on the brink of hell,
    Their endless torment sealed.

Their sins arrayed before them rise
    Like mountains tall and great;
Their past life how they now despise,
    Deplore their dying state.

They cannot walk, they cannot stand,
    Their trembling form gives way,
And sinking down with lifted hands,
    In earnestness they pray.

At last they feel their sins forgiven,
    Their burdened souls set free,

And in their hearts a hope of heaven
  Springs up eternally.

The gospel trumpet leads the way.
  It gives a joyful sound,
It finds poor children gone astray,
  By it the lost are found.

They find their thirsting souls refreshed,
  Their daily drink and meat;
O happy day, the gospel brought,
  Salvation, O how sweet.

They seem to cheerish and to prize,
  True happiness within;
O how they long to be baptized,
  And quit the paths of sin.

The gladsome tidings, glorious news,
  Brings children lost, to sight;
No child of God can well refuse
  The day instead of night.

118. C. M.
Departed Friends.

Why should we fear the time to die?
  Or mourn our dearest friends?
When from this world their souls shall fly,
  Their earthly trouble ends.

Why should we grieve or shed a tear,
  Or let sorrow fill the heart?
For well we know that death is near,
  From earth we soon shall part.

What could we find in this poor world,
    That we should wish to stay?
So many trials, pains and tears,
    Are found along the way.

This sinful life will soon be o'er,
    Our time of grief and pain,
And we shall reach a blessed shore,
    Washed clean from every stain.

Why should we fear the time to die?
    Or take our last farewell?
To join our friends in brighter skies,
    In heavenly lands to dwell.

Why should we mourn for dearest friends,
    When called from this dull shore?
For them all sin and sorrow ends,
    And afflictions pain no more.

119.
Greater Peace of Mind.

O for a greater peace of mind,
    While dwelling here below;
While serving out our precious time,
    Let love and friendship grow.

Let new desires and fonder hopes
    Burst forth from day to day;
Spring up like tender plants that grow,
    Spread beauty along the way.

A crown of everlasting joy,
    Shines forth like morning light;

Faith, love and hope our minds employ,
  Our every-day delight.

120.   S. M.
Love.

In union there is bliss,
  In hearts together wove;
What mutual binding tie is this,
  The fellowship of love!

Our tender, throbbing hearts,
  Once more are filled with love,
A cordial greeting each imparts,
  A token from above.

O let our joys abound
  In sweetest melody,
In rapturous praise, end all our days,
  From worldly pleasures flee.

Let every tear be dry,
  The tender cords be healed;
For every spot where love has touched,
  A brother's sigh will feel.

121.   C. M.
Sheep Abroad.

We read the writing on the wall,
  The finger board of God,
And there we find the way for all
  Poor strangers found abroad.

While traveling in some distant land,
 And left without a guide,
Out on the rocks or treacherous sand,
 In danger of the tide.

Our Savior seeks there for His sheep,
 The little lambs that cry;
When loud and long He calls for them,
 They only groan and sigh.

Oh, would they all but come to Him,
 Be housed within His walls,
Be fed by His own skillful hand,
 And answer when He calls.

122.   7s.
Our Gloomy Life.

Deep in sorrows and in sin,
 Distresses around me lie;
O what is life, or what is gain?
 Or who will answer when I cry?

Dark and lonely is the way,
 All along life's troubled stream;
Anxious thoughts rise day by day;
 To live and die, is it a dream?

Trembling beneath a load of sin,
 Grief, and woe, and many tears;
Often asking, Is there a God?
 Almost hopeless the way appears.

Life's brittle thread it soon must break,
 Death's solemn hour we soon must face;

And then we'll beg for mercy's sake,
    O then we'll ask for dying grace.

123.   L. M.
            The Apostle Paul.

The Apostle Paul, from error to save,
    The quickened Gentiles sought to win;
And with the gospel, true and brave,
    He faced the storms of wicked men.

He turned them from the dark to light,
    That they, with opened eyes, might see,
Receive the truth as well as sight,
    And from their idol worship flee.

The middle wall was broken down,
    The nations all could enter in;
Christ Jesus was the Rising Sun,
    Their dark, cold, heathen hearts to win.

The apostle labored night and day,
    He faced the heat and stinging cold;
In heathen lands, though dark the way,
    He pled with sinners, young and old.

He cared not for the angry beasts,
    Nor for the viper's poisonous bite;
He taught the greatest and the least,
    That Jesus was their Living Light.

124.   8s. 6s.
            With Christ Above.

We soon shall leave this house of clay,
    For one eternal, endless day,

Where saints immortal ever stay,
   In a fair world above;
O could we see our Savior's face,
Before we reach the heavenly place,
Or view the shining world of grace,
   The mansions full of love!

O then I'd doubt and fear no more,
Till my poor soul could onward soar,
To Canaan's fair and blissful shore,
   Forever there to rest;
There bathe my soul in that fair clime
Where all the holy angels shine,
Throughout one long and endless time,
   In perfect union blest.

There join our hearts in love to sing
Of Jesus Christ our heavenly King,
And let our voices ever ring,
   In sweetest melody;
There sound His praise through endless days,
For all his righteous, perfect ways,
And every moment there will praise,
   Through all eternity.

We'll cast our crowns before Him there,
In that bright world so pure and fair,
For God and Christ are always near,
   Forever to remain;
There'll be one long and peaceful rest,
Where children are forever blest,
And numbered with the royal guest,
   We'll join in glad refrain.

125.

Our Desire.

The light, O Lord, let shine,
   From heaven's radiant shore;
Light up my poor, benighted mind,
   Till it will ask no more.

All troubles did depart,
   Then let me calmly rest;
Abide with me and fill my heart,
   Then I'll be surely blest.

I'll rise then from my couch,
   My pillow bathed in tears,
And from my soul proclaim enough
   Of joy in after years.

My soul be fed on love,
   And evermore will sing,
My thoughts, exalted, soar above
   In triumph with my King.

My race is almost run,
   The days all past and gone;
I cannot check the setting sun,
   Nor stop my traveling on.

O Lord, if I am thine,
   Then let my soul soon rest,
Along the shores of endless time,
   Forever with the blest.

And ever there remain,
   In thy great courts above,

Where Jesus will forever reign,
  All troubles drowned in love.

Great rivers there will flow,
  Of joy, peace and love,
No more hard trials e'er can know,
  For there'll be none above.

126.   C. M.
          To Be Born Again.

God's holy spirit surely finds,
  No matter where we roam,
We can't resist the light that shines
  In our benighted homes.

Who would refuse the gift of God?
  Or break the silver chain,
Connecting with the land above,
  That land without a stain?

Refuse the gift! poor man of flesh,
  Resist the power of God!
None can resist, no, never, one
  Hath yet withstood His word.

But if a child come to the birth
  Can resist being born,
We might resist the power of God,
  And stay His mighty arm.

Religion is a precious prize,
  A charm without a stain;
It comes from God, down from the skies,
  A prize we love to claim.

A welcome message from above,
  One we delight to hear;
It fills a throbbing heart with love,
  And gives the hearing ear.

127.   7s. 6s.

Thanksgiving Day.

Thanksgiving day brings gladness,
  With its overflowing bowl,
That drives away all sadness,
  And feeds the hungry soul;
Then thousands feast on blessings,
  The good things of the land,
The Lord's mercy all confessing,
  In all their social band.

When round the table gathered,
  With dainties rich and rare,
They should the Lord remember,
  Who sends their daily share;
When loaded down with fatness,
  That comes up from the ground,
Remember 'tis God's goodness
  That sends all blessings down.

We know full well our weakness,
  By nature sin defiled,
Although we hope not thankless,
  For blessings all the while;
Be grateful for his goodness,
  Throughout the live-long day;

We know full well His riches,
  From Him the great display.

He clothes the earth with plenty,
  'Tis scattered all around,
That none should be left empty,
  If love 'mong all be found;
But while we all feel thankful,
  For what our Father gives,
How can we be contented,
  If our brother scarcely lives.

While the Lord is sending riches,
  And there's plenty at the door,
We ought to feel contented,
  And feed the hungry poor;
When all have done their duty,
  In scattering things around,
They can rightly thank the giver,
  For sending blessings down.

128.   8s. 7s.

The Grave.

All the world is traveling onward,
  From the cradle to the grave;
All are marching swiftly forward,
  And in the dust will soon be laid;
Rich and poor lie down together,
  Side by side, lie in the ground;
There the rich will fare no better,
  There they'll wear no brighter crown.

Cold and silent, dust and ashes,
    All their bodies turned to clay,
Mix and mingle there together,
    Till the resurrection day.
In the grave they'll no more weary,
    Winds and storms no longer fright;
No more days so dark and dreary,
    All is one long, unknown night.

Kings and princes with their riches,
    All their forms to fade away;
Jewels bright, and shining diamonds,
    Lie beneath the silent clay;
Wicked men and crying children,
    Hastening onward to the tomb—
Countless thousands still are marching
    To the grave, their lonely home.

Sleep on, nations, with your millions,
    Rest beneath the cold, cold ground;
Rest on there for God is reigning,
    Till they hear the trumpet sound;
Jesus Christ again is coming,
    Saint and sinner, will you hear?
All will arise, and all behold Him;
    Don't you know that day is near?

129.   C. M.

Wandering Children.

Look down, look down, Almighty God,
    Behold Thy scattered sons;

O call them gently by Thy word,
   Poor, wandering little ones.

Out in a stormy desert land,
   Thy wandering children roam;
A deceitful world extends its hand,
   Inviting them to come.

'Midst turmoils and confusions great,
   They wander among the dead;
While dwelling with the desolate
   They're hungering for bread.

In some far distant land they dwell,
   And languish, mourn and pine;
The mighty hosts of men do tell
   These strangers are not Thine.

Their Father's house has bread to spare,
   And honey, milk and wine;
There they can eat and drink and share
   The gifts of God to Zion.

In gospel lands sweet angels dwell,
   And in the church there's room,
So sweetly whispering all do tell,
   Dear, wandering child, come home.

Distinctly hear the watchman's voice,
   The gospel trumpet sound,
So calmly, sweetly all rejoice,
   When wandering children come.

Out in the grumbling, growling world,
   Thy children ofttimes go;

But out in the darkest night is heard,
  Dear, wandering child, come home.

Come all ye weak and lowly saints,
  Who find no rest abroad,
Come tell us of your worst complaints,
  Come to the church of God.

Come, O come, dear child, come home,
  We hear your Savior say,
Come with your ills and bleeding wounds,
  He'll wipe them all away.

130.   C. M.
A Rotten Ball.

We look upon this glowing earth,
  This great, uneven plain,
And see a world of restless men,
  Who're seeking worldly gain.

We see their dreadful days of old
  Stretched out beyond control,
Along life's dark and hidden ways,
  A stream of crime unfold.

O stormy looks the road ahead;
  Poor, suffering worms are we,
So crooked is the way we tread,
  O'er this unfathomed sea.

There's piles on piles of rubbish here,
  Seen almost everywhere;
And in the forms of human flesh,
  Sink down to ruin here.

There's murder, theft and wicked lies,
    And midnight screams of men,
There's nothing good before their eyes,
    A world of sickening sin.

An unsound ball of human flesh,
    That's festering to the core;
Yet onward to the goal they rush,
    A putrefying sore.

We wonder and we stand amazed,
    At this great moving sight,
A foaming sea, that's rolling high,
    Their brightest day is night.

From whence come they? and whither go?
    This sea of human will?
Rivers of men, like streams that flow,
    And never standing still.

Yet roll the mighty torrents past,
    Bewildered throngs depend,
On self rely unto the last,
    Unto their bitter end.

131.   C. M.
With God.

God is the theme of all our joys,
    In Him our hopes all blend;
Our words, our works, our minds employed.
    Against all sin contend.

O let our minds flow out in peace,
    And grace our souls adorn,

Delivered from all worldliness,
    And sin of every form.

Beneath the shadow of His wings,
    Our new life will be sweet;
And joy and peace, salvation brings,
    When sitting at His feet.

132.   7s.
Serving Out Our Time.

We all are serving out our time,
    From the cradle to the grave;
Foes we make, and friends we find,
    Borne to us on every wave.

On the waters, night and day,
    Ofttimes deep and angry, too,
Paddling o'er the boisterous way,
    In our frail and weak canoe.

O we dread the route ahead,
    Covered up in mist and gloom;
All this life is full of dread,
    Oft its ending comes at noon.

Fears of torment round us lie,
    O we dread the dangerous shoals;
We must work, and watch and pray,
    While the billows round us roll.

We're all serving out our time
    In this cold, beclouded night;
But 'cross the angry waves there shines
    Further on a cheering light.

133. 8s. 6s.
Gospel for All.

Lift up, O Lord, lift from the dead,
  That all may stand erect,
The little lambs be humbly fed,
  Thine own peculiar sect.

'Mong every nation, land or tongue,
  Wherever they are found,
May Thy peculiar, zealous ones,
  Feed on the gospel sound.

To all the gospel word is sent,
  All nations far and nigh;
The apostles to dark regions went,
  And made a plaintive cry.

Reprove, convince, convert and teach,
  The Gentile and the Jew;
Exhort, admonish and beseech,
  To turn and live anew.

134. L. M.
The Song of Love.

This lovely earth I'd like to see,
Without its crime and misery;
All nature would be clothed in smiles,
If man was pure and undefiled.

There'd be no pestilence nor plague,
If man had lived as he was made;
There'd be no curse upon the ground,
If sin in man had not been found.

There'd be no cold, or heat or storm,
If man was free from sin and harm;
Summer would last throughout the year,
And heaven on earth at once appear.

But, O great God, now we behold,
Man's sins like torrents round him roll,
Go rushing like a mighty wind—
To change the man, who can begin?

The man is lost, and deaf, and blind;
While dead in sins, how can he find?
And without strength he can't obey;
No love for God, how can he pray?

And without faith he cannot please,
From head to foot he is diseased;
How can a healing balm be found,
When such deadly sins abound?

The work of love, at last begun,
Then man repents of every wrong;
A righteous God with grace appears,
And wipes away the falling tears.

The Lord adorns the naked soul,
And wraps it round with vestures whole;
In every land and every tongue,
The song of love, let it be sung.

135.   C. M.

Born to Die.

Does Jesus know we're wandering home,
   All foot-sore, faint and worn?

Does Jesus know we're traveling on,
    All bleeding, bruised and torn?

We come in tears and go in tears,
    In tears we wend our way;
We're born in sin, and live in sin,
    In sin both night and day.

We're traveling on, for we must die,
    Our hearts distressed within;
We cannot tell the causes why,
    Unless it be for sin.

We cannot drive away our fears,
    Nor from the grim monster fly;
We cannot dry up all our tears,
    For we are born to die.

136.   C. M.
Erring Sons.

God in the riches of His grace,
    Hath taught His erring sons;
Down in their hearts His law He placed,
    For their own good 'twas done.

God, in the riches of His grace,
    Hath opened wide the door,
That they might enter in, and taste
    His mercies evermore.

The richest fruits are strewn around
    For them to feed upon;
And they the healthy food may take,
    Rejoice and grow thereon.

But there are ever tempting snares,
    And traps about their feet,
Which often catch them unawares,
    And their destruction meet.

Reject all tithes and offerings made,
    Lest they should rob the Lord,
Return unto the Lord of Hosts,
    Be guided by His word.

137.   L. M.
The Straight Way.

Straight is the way I'd like to find,
But nature is so bad inclined;
O what I would I cannot do,
I would to God I could be true.

O I'm so faint, so weak and poor,
I cannot make myself secure;
I lay my body down to rest,
And pray the Lord to make me blest.

The yoke I'd wear, and gladly, too,
No better course could I pursue;
But sins pile up around me high,
I'm prone to sin as sparks to fly.

To find the way I'll try again,
While here on earth I still remain;
And if through grace I can believe,
I'll ask of God and help receive.

I would recall the days gone by,
Perhaps you know the reason why;

But still I must depend on grace,
For I could not the right way trace.

I'll go to Jesus with my load,
Perhaps He'll keep me in the road;
I'll pray God keep my heart inclined
To search His word the path to find.

138.   7s.
Desire to Be Reconciled.

O could I be prepared to die,
That poor soul be lifted high;
In the green pastures of God's love,
My soul to dwell with Him above!

But O, my soul is sick and poor,
And drawing near to death's dark door;
Weak and wounded, halt and lame,
Here on earth I still remain.

Sad and lonely are my days,
I cannot hope to mend my ways;
Truly God to me is kind,
Calms and soothes my troubled mind.

Many are my lonesome days,
Life is dull without God's grace,
Waiting on in my distress,
All my faults I do confess.

O could I be prepared to die,
Reconciled my soul to fly!
Be prepared of God to go,
Reconciled while here below!

139. C. M.

'Tis Sweet to Meet.

If love be planted in the breast,
    And knit around the heart,
'Tis sweet to meet, in union rest,
    But parting has its smart.

'Tis sweet, when we our minds employ,
    Together all as one;
Our bosoms swell with inward joy,
    Our time salvation's won.

'Tis sweet to meet our brethren dear,
    And unite our ardent prayers;
Where love flows out and is sincere,
    It drowns all worldly cares.

'Tis sweet to meet the saints below,
    Each one a joy to bring,
Where love like streams of water flow;
    But parting has its sting.

140. 7s.

Song.

Just and holy, pure and kind,
    Is the righteous God we find;
Wondrous love and power combined,
    Always in one frame of mind.

Just as sure as the waters roll,
    As sure as they fall and run;
Just that sure he will control
    All beneath the shining sun.

All the shining lights will fail,
  Mountains tremble shake and fall;
He'll perform and do his will,
  He is King and Lord of all.

Omnipotence all these did make,
  All arranged by this great power,
Rivers, seas and distant lands,
  All brought forth in one still hour.

O when the Lord declares the end,
  Worlds of men before him stand;
Need they ask Him why or when?
  All must wait His great command.

He's not under their control,
  Nor is swayed by skill or slight;
He will govern and will rule,
  And will always do the right.

Education, art nor skill,
  All the earth's great learned minds.
Could e'er overthrow His will,
  Nor can change His bright designs.

All the earthly powers combined,
  Could not change His sacred law.
He is always in one mind,
  And will all His people draw.

All the morals of this world
  Fade and vanish out of sight,
When compared to His dear Son—
  He's the bright and shining light.

O that we loved as we were loved,
    When our Savior died for men,
When He left the courts above,
    To buy us back to God again.

But we may trust in His great name,
    His grace and mercy lean upon,
Though we are fallen creatures still,
    And in sins will still go on.

We are frail, and weak, and poor,
    And through self can't hope to gain;
Jesus is the way and door,
    Let us hope through Him to reign.

141.   8s. 6s.

The Unseen God.

O'er all this earth, in heaven there dwells,
    An unseen, living God;
And every act of man He tells,
    And places on record.

With watchful and unsleeping eyes,
    Our every pathway's seen,
And every trick before Him lies,
    At every place we've been.

We place our feet on slippery ground,
    And wallow in the mire;
All filthy specks and spots are found,
    For God doth never tire.

Our course, when guided by the mind,
    That seeks a worldly share,

Oft unbecoming places find,
    And many cumbering cares.

At every spot and place man goes,
    God's watchful eyes are there,
And every deed and act He sees,
    And every falling hair.

142.   8s. 7s.
He Will Save Us.

We are drifting, swiftly drifting,
    From the cradle to the grave,
While the winds go softly whispering,
    We are asking, Who will save?
God will save us if we trust Him,
    Trust with faith and are sincere,
For His ears are ever open,
    He will always kindly hear.

We feel wearied, poor and needy,
    As to works we're very bare,
What we have are poor and scanty,
    And for them God doth not care.
But we'll try to cleanse our garments—
    May we the cleansing fountain find—
But for works He will not own us,
    They must all be left behind.

If in form only we're serving,
    And our thoughts are all impure,
Not for works will God accept us,
    They are poor, at best, I'm sure.

If we're asking, ever asking,
    Without faith, 'tis all in vain;
Not for doing will he crown us,
    We for works ne'er heaven can gain.

We are walking and we're halting,
    Filled with doubts and many fears;
If we're filled with faith and trusting,
    He will wipe away all tears.
God is pure, and good and holy,
    He is just and not unfair;
If we love Him and obey Him,
    He will then to us draw near.

Jesus Christ is our Redeemer,
    He that saved us from our sins;
'Twas through love that He redeemed us,
    And by grace draws us to Him;
Jesus Christ is our dear Savior,
    And He will His mercies send;
We will trust Him and adore Him,
    He will save us in the end.

143.   L M.

The World.

O what is all this world to me
With all its crime and misery?
The way of life is dark and cold,
The depths of sin to me unfold.

O what is all this world to me,
With all its wants and poverty?

Deception's taught with pomp and pride,
The gates of hell are open wide.

O what is all this world to me,
With all its cold formality?
I cannot love the man of sin,
I hate the paths that he walks in.

O what is all this world to me?
All it can give is vanity;
Polluted streams on earth here flow,
Their surging tides still onward go.

O what is all this world to me,
With all its show and great display?
It can't console nor feed my mind,
No soothing balm here can I find.

O what is all this world to me?
From it, O Lord, I would be free;
Prepare me for a better home,
Beyond this sin-stained land, to come.

144.   7s.
Draw Me Closer.

Draw me closer, closer, Lord,
Let me hover round Thy word;
Let me shelter 'neath Thy wing,
Closer to Thy cross I'd cling.

Let me ask of Thee, and find
Greater love and peace of mind;
When I through fiery trials wade,
Be my shelter and my shade.

Help me to improve my ways,
Teach and keep me all my days;
Come, O come, and dwell with me,
Or let me come and live with Thee.

Let me count up all the cost,
Wear the yoke and bear the cross;
Let me with my feet and face,
Humbly walk in every place.

Hear my prayer and tune my song;
Turn my steps when they'd go wrong;
Let not too heavy be my cross,
Cleanse my heart of every dross.

Draw me closer, closer, Lord,
Let me hear Thy gentle word;
Soothe and calm my troubled breast,
Let me in Thy bosom rest.

In the fleeting earth-life hours,
Let me feel Thy cleansing powers;
In my last expiring breath,
Let me claim Thee mine in death.

145. 8s. 6s.

Death.

O man, O man, thou wilt depart,
 Wilt lose thy shape and form;
The beating pulse and throbbing heart
 Wilt never more return.

The tongue forget its part to bear,
 The eyes be closed in sleep,

The ears will then forget to hear,
    The soul no longer weep.

The arms will then refuse to move,
    The feet refuse to walk,
The lips turn pale, be stiff, and cold
    In death, no longer talk.

'Tis right! 'Tis right! for God hath said,
    The soul comes back to Him;
Why should we fear, or longer dread,
    If Christ our souls did win?

146.   8s. 7s.
In Memory of a Departed Brother.

O farewell, my loving brother,
    O farewell—a last adieu;
God has called thee, high up yonder,
    Thou wast faithful, kind and true.

CHORUS:
    Fare thee well, fare thee well,
    Fare thee well, my loving brother,
    I must bid a last adieu.

Years and years we'll sorrow after,
    For our hearts are stung with pain;
In this life we part forever,
    But we hope to meet again.

CHO.—

Many days and weeks thou'st lingering,
    Sick and sad with grief and pain;

Thou art gone and left us mourning,
    But we hope to meet again.

Cho.—

Thou hast gone and left us weeping,
    Poor and lonely we here remain;
But we'll trust in our dear Savior,
    And shall hope to meet again.

Cho.—

Sad and lonely we are waiting
    For the Lord to call us home;
We are standing at the crossing,
    Waiting for the word to come.

Cho.—

Many years have we been traveling,
    And our journey's almost through;
We have found that all are fading,
    Soon we'll be in heaven with you.

Cho.—

Soon the chill of death will catch us,
    Then how soon will all be o'er!
When we cross the angry river
    We shall meet to part no more.

Cho.—

147.   S. M.

On the Rolling Wave.

How small, how small, am I,
    Out on this restless sea;

I'm floating on the rolling waves,
  All helpless I seem to be.

I'm borne by every breeze,
  Both high and low I go;
I ofttimes feel I'm sinking down,
  Deep in the depths below.

But when there comes a calm,
  I quickly spread my sail;
'Tis then I see just what I am,
  So soon begin to fail.

Borne on by every wind,
  Just like a floating ball,
'Tis here, and there, and everywhere,
  No safe retreat at all.

I'm carried with the tide,
  To where, I know not, now;
The little speck of clay must glide,
  No safe retreat at all.

Could I but safely ride,
  To some fair port ahead,
Entrust myself with one that saves,
  O then I should not dread.

148.   C. M.
Come to Christ and Drink.

O come, poor, sick and wounded man,
  Come tell us your complaint;
Poor, thirsting, trembling, fainting soul,
  O come to Christ and drink.

O come, poor, hungry, doubting one,
    And He'll most freely give;
The Great Physician bids you come,
    O come, and drink, and live.

For inquiring souls, who love the Lord,
    A cup of joy is found;
A peaceful home is your reward,
    A balm for every wound.

'Tis living men who thirst and mourn,
    And living men who pray;
'Tis living men who hear the word,
    And humbly ask the way.

O come, poor, sinful, weeping soul,
    Poor, wounded, ready to sink;
O come, poor child, and be made whole,
    O come to Christ and drink.

149.   8s. 7s.

Day is Breaking.

Day is breaking, day is breaking,
    Once again the light appears;
We are waiting, we are waiting,
    For the rising sun is near;
O the sky will soon be clearing,
    All the clouds will break away;
Day is breaking, day is breaking,
    We are waiting for the day.

Life is fading, life is fading,
    All are marching to the tomb;

All are going, all are going,
　Tender blossoms just in bloom;
'Round us gathering,'round us gathering,
　Death is gathering closer by;
O the sickle, O the sickle,
　Soon will hush the children's cry.

Poor and needy, poor and needy,
　Weak and wounded, sore and lame;
We are waiting, we are waiting,
　For the land without a stain;
We are waiting, we are waiting,
　For the breaking of the day;
All are waiting for that morning,
　When the clouds will pass away.

Cheer up, loved ones, cheer up, loved ones;
　Jesus is that lovely morn;
Look unto Him, look unto Him,
　He will all your souls adorn;
Cheer up, dear ones, cheer up, dear ones;
　Soon the clouds will break away.
We are waiting, we are waiting,
　We are waiting for that day.

150.　　　　　　　　　　　　C. M.

Experience.

My mind goes back to yonder place
　Where the small cottage stood,
The very spot where I once lay,
　Close by the silent wood.

For many days and weeks I lay,
  With burning fevers low;
How did I bear from day to day
  This dreadful, dreadful foe?

With fevers, chills and pains throughout,
  My days were rolling on,
'Till my poor soul was moved to doubt,
  And almost to despond.

At last I found a lisping prayer,
  From my poor heart arise;
My sins piled up now everywhere,
  And them I so despised.

I tried to pray as best I could,
  Distresses round me lay;
With every breath I prayed to God,
  In my poor, sinful way.

My aching heart felt weighted down
  With some great, heavy load;
As though some great rock laid thereon,
  And which I could not move.

In this dread strain, with grief and fear,
  In anguish I had lain;
My body, too, was sinking down,
  With ills, and aches, and pain.

In this great trial of my life,
  While death seemed lingering near,
I called on God with all my might;
  He did not seem to hear.

I called for one good brother there,
    While I was so distressed;
I hoped that God his prayer would hear,
    And then I would be blessed.

I could not cast the load away,
    My hope had almost flown;
My wickedness I plainly saw,
    The vile seed I had sown.

I turned my face unto the wall,
    In grief and sad despair;
And while my eyes were closed in sleep,
    God surely blessed me there.

My aches and ills and pains were gone,
    And I was then made whole,
And could not with my tongue portray,
    The happiness of my soul.

'Twas there I felt the load remove,
    The sin which I despised;
And there I felt a love for God,
    And wished to be baptized.

151.   8s.

My Poor Ways.

O, I'm so poor, so cold and blind,
How can I change my roving mind,
And turn to God with all my heart,
And bid all sin from me depart?

My heart feels often froze within,
I feel I'm buried deep in sin;

How can I with my mind control
The wicked way that grieves my soul?

How can I walk the narrow way,
And find a safer place to stay?
O could I find some smoother road,
To travel on towards my God?

I am so weak and sin-defiled,
I feel I'm guilty all the while;
So oft in darkness all the day,
I'm lost in sin and can't obey.

I've found my nature all unclean,
Proceeding from a wicked stream;
Corrupt and filthy waters flow,
From nature's fountain here below.

Unyielding is my natural mind,
So deep in sin, few joys I find,
And so I travel, day by day,
I'm ofttimes led so far astray.

O could I turn my face to God,
And hover near His sacred word,
And shelter 'neath His lovely wings,
And rest content with richer things.

I'd turn my back on this gay world,
And live to gain a brighter pearl;
I'd follow Jesus every day,
And strive to walk the narrow way.

Then I could find much sweeter rest,
Where I could be forever blest;

I'd tell of Christ and praise His grace,
And walk with Him in every place.

152.   C. M.

A Dark and Cloudy Day.

O let these lonely hours go by,
   As fast as they can run;
A dreary mist obscures the sky,
   And we are all undone.

Cast down in sorrow and in sin,
   Distresses round us lie;
O what is life, or where is gain?
   Or who will hear my cry?

How dark and lonely is the way,
   Along life's troubled stream!
When anxious thoughts day after day,
   But little hope can glean.

O let the moments swiftly pass,
   May light shine from above;
And give us faith, O Lord, to rest,
   In thy strong arms of love.

153.   C. M.

God is Everywhere.

'Mongst all the scattered tribes of men,
   God's mercy there is shown;
No matter why, or where, or when,
   He'll make His wishes known.

For He is God and souls will find,
   No matter where they be; .

For He is loving, good and kind,
    From all eternity.

Out in the silent, endless space,
    With earth revolving round,
He hides from us a smiling face,
    But everywhere He's found.

He fixed the moon and starry lights,
    To shine upon us here;
He dwells below and in the heights,
    For God is everywhere.

Among the high and towering hills,
    Along the crooked streams,
At any place, and every place,
    His mighty works are seen.

And far away in distant lands,
    He plants His footsteps there;
His track is left upon the sands,
    For God is everywhere.

When far out in the silent woods,
    Where man has seldom trod,
Among the tall and lofty trees,
    There, too, we find our God.

And on the wild and dreary plains,
    As well as in the air,
No place is found but there he reigns,
    For God is everywhere.

Beneath the scorching, sultry sun,
    Or at the frigid zone,

Wherever man's disposed to run,
　　God surely there is known.

He moves the rolling wheels of time,
　　And guides the earth with care,
In all the world, in every clime,
　　For God is everywhere.

He rides upon the bursting storm,
　　That breaks upon the land;
He takes the tempest in his arm,
　　And guides it with his hand.

And every wind by Him is borne,
　　Although at times severe;
But He will make His power known,
　　For God is everywhere.

There's no place found on this broad earth,
　　No spot that we might see,
There's not a place that we could find,
　　But God will always be.

No matter where or when we go,
　　We should always walk with care,
Be careful what we say and do,
　　For God is everywhere.

L. M.

Experience.

'Twas eighteen hundred and sixty-five
When first I felt my soul alive;
'Twas then I first began to pray,
'Twas then I first sought out the way.

Pray let me tell just how it came.
I was weak and wounded, sore and lame,
In darkness and in doubtful mind,
No rest nor soothing balm could find.

O what a load was bearing down!
A world of sin in me was found!
My flesh was weak and full of pain,
I sought and asked, but all in vain.

My empty heart was hard as stone,
And nothing good had I ever done;
I longed and cried, great moanings made;
At every breath I humbly prayed.

For days and weeks I thus complained,
Till God relieved me from my pain;
'Twas grace that taught me what to say,
'Twas grace that led my soul to pray.

A battle fought, a victory won,
When God revealed His only Son;
My mind was overflowing, full,
Great joy and peace then filled my soul.

I love the same still, tender voice,
That made my soul then so rejoice;
I love to tell the live-long day,
That Jesus led me in the way.

O what is man without his God
To lead him safely o'er the road,
And teach and show him all his sins?
'Tis then his praying life begins.

155. C. M.
Death.
(A SICK DAY. JAN. 25, 1897.)

The angry storm of death is near,
　A threatening, dangerous gale;
And our poor boat is dashed about;
　How shall we longer sail?

We're bending low before the wind,
　Soon we'll be dashed aground;
Our sails all mangled by the storm,
　In bad condition found.

We're yielding to the conquering foe,
　How quick we're in His arms!
Death gains the victory here below,
　It has no lovely charms.

A distant light doth shine afar,
　Beyond this sinking wall;
With heaven's beautiful gate ajar,
　We'll gladly welcome all.

Our victory lies beyond this night,
　When angry storms are past;
Once o'er the hills we'll reach the light,
　The victory gained at last.

156. C. M.
He Comes.

O see, the clouds are scattering fast,
　And rushing through the air;
Go tell the world that Jesus Christ
　Will shortly now appear.

Come, O come, King Jesus, come,
    The judgment day appears;
Descending from His Father's throne,
    He'll wipe away all tears.

It is the children of the light,
    The children of the day,
And not the children of the night,
    That He will take away.

From every cliff, and mountain top,
    And valley, far and near.
The rivers, and the seas give up,
    His tender lambs with care.

They'll meet their Savior in the air
    With one continuous shout;
There'll be no suffering, pain or fear,
    No longer be a doubt.

For Jesus Christ will come to bless
    And take His people home,
Forever more with Him they'll rest,
    Around the great white throne.

157.   L. M.

Our Lustful Eyes.

The blustering winds and frowning skies
Give warning to our lustful eyes;
We're pushed along and moved about,
Found traveling o'er the crooked route.

O how we long and wish to say
That we have found some better way;

We live, and hope, and hope in vain,
Our spirit life seems almost slain.

O could we climb Mount Zion's hill,
And satisfy our inward will,
We'd walk with saints along the streets,
And view the fold our Shepherd keeps.

We'd go in and out at His command,
Be fruitful in the promised land;
And at our feet a lamp would shine,
That lights the way to a heavenly clime.

We'd live to adorn the gospel way,
In living fields from day to day;
We'd magnify the heavenly law,
And sweeter comfort from it draw.

We'd talk and walk from hill to hill,
With brighter joys our souls would fill;
We'd break away from sinful ties,
If we were free from lustful eyes.

158. 8s. 7s.
We Long For Rest.

We are watching and we're trembling,
   Along this dark and lonely way;
Many more sad hearts are lingering,
   Waiting for the coming day;
Life is but a dreary wending,
   All is vain that goes for show,
All will come to one sad ending,
   Death will deal the stinging blow.

Though the world is roaring loudly,
   Yet it's traveling on at ease;
Step by step it's marching proudly,
   In its vernal life of peace;
But I'm sinking down in sorrow,
   My poor heart is filled with gloom,
I am watching for the morrow,
   When I'll be carried to the tomb.

Many friends have crossed the valley,
   To the bright and sun-lit sky;
And there's many thousands crossing,
   To that glory-world on high;
Millions, millions gone on shouting,
   They have crossed the Jordan o'er;
Many weary hearts still beating,
   For the endless summer shore.

All will join in singing anthems,
   O, dear soul, dismiss thy fears,
Christ the Lord is our great Captain,
   Trembling sinners, dry your tears;
When we reach the golden city,
   Find the shadows blown away,
There we'll find a lasting greeting,
   In that fair, eternal day.

159.   C. M.
Heaven.

In heaven no gallant ships go by.
   Nor prowling sinners rove;

No suffering children there will cry,
    For all up there is love.

No winters, and no chilling winds,
    No dark and cloudy days,
But when the heavenly day begins,
    Decembers change to Mays.

It's not for gold that we may sing.
    Hallelujahs up on high;
It's not for pay that heaven will ring,
    That bright and cloudless sky.

It's not a place where wizzards live,
    Or devils take a part;
It's not for gold that we receive,
    Or get the change of heart.

The devils act, and move, and pray,
    But not for heaven's home;
Of it they do not care to say,
    Or speak of its high dome.

'Tis only here, and of their gold.
    It's all they seem to care;
Always are doubting when they're told
    Of heaven's home so fair.

The ragged urchins of the street,
    On India's coral shore,
May fare the best, and they may meet
    An open, friendly door.

May find a royal diadem,
    And diamond crowns to wear,

While devils and all wicked men,
    Can never enter there.

'Twas not designed for men of wealth,
    And men of great renown,
To curse and swear at every breath,
    And then to wear a crown.

'Tis only for the pure in heart,
    The loved ones of the Lord;
All others God will bid depart,
    Who did not mind His word.

Christ is the green and living tree,
    The true and living vine,
And none can ever heaven see,
    Who did not Jesus find.

160.   8s. 7s.

Thankful.

Thankful for all blessings rendered,
    Saints should thank the Lord always,
All their daily thanks be tendered,
    They should so devote their days,
For such gracious gifts bestowing;
    Every blade of grass that's green.
Every shrub and plant that's growing,
    All their blessings come from Him.

Thankful for the air they're breathing,
    Thankful to their God always,
Thankful for each crumb receiving,
    Thanks to Him throughout their days;

Thankful for the rain descending,
   And the stars that give the light,
While their fondest hopes are dreaming,
   In the darkness of the night.

Oft they bow before Him, trembling,
   Wayward children 'neath the sky,
On their knees before Him bending,
   Guilty worms before Him sigh;
Their rich bounty from Him's flowing,
   To His saints in little bands,
Thanks to Him for food that's growing,
   Thanks to Him for home and lands.

On Him surely they're depending,
   May they walk with thankful hearts;
For His grace and love unending,
   They should bid all sin depart;
While His favors they are courting,
   May they learn of Him and know,
He's so freely them supporting,
   That at His feet they humbly bow.

For all needful daily blessings,
   Thankful souls to God should go;
In the midst of undeservings
   He freely feeds them all below;
For the many favors giving,
   They should thank the Lord always,
End their days in humble praising,
   Thankful souls so end their days.

161.   8s. 6s.

In the World.

All men are tossed and whirled about,
　Like straws before the wind,
They all are hurried in and out,
　For all alike have sinned.

Like forest leaves that fade and fall,
　Their life is short, you know;
A chilling wind soon strikes them all,
　And scatters them below.

Poor, begging, creeping worms are we,
　In nature's ugly fold;
The winding of humanity,
　In nature dark and cold.

Why is it thus, or who could tell,
　Or hath the power to know?
Or if for bad, or if for well,
　How strangely thus and so.

We somehow trust that for our good,
　A cleansing stream may flow,
And wash the defects from our blood,
　And make us white as snow.

But O, we know not anything.
　As we would wish to know.
About the source from which it springs,
　Or the course its waters go.

My thoughts run thus, my mind runs full,
　I'm crying all the night,

A feeble, moaning, waning cry,
    With only hope for sight.

I walk with tired, halting feet,
    I'm blindly limping on;
How can I, with my nature, keep
    The law, or life adorn?

How foolish is an aimless mind;
    An aimless tongue to talk;
An aimless tongue to direct the blind,
    Or aimless feet to walk.

Our God, He dwells in heaven above,
    As clean and white as snow;
He does not aimless, walk or move,
    Nor ask of us to know.

O let us then all trust in Him,
    He'll cleanse us through and through,
Wash the defects from our blood,
    And make us all anew.

162.   L. M.

Parental Home.

We walk around our parent's home,
We place our feet where smiles once come;
We rested 'neath our parent's care,
For they were faithful and sincere.

The summer came with passing days,
Our time was spent in youthful ways;
We traveled on with months and years,
But soon we found our home in tears.

God took our parents from us away
And left us by ourselves to stay;
Most solemn thoughts impress the mind—
A lonely place here now we find.

The sunshine of the past is gone,
And we are traveling faster on;
While mist and gloom obscure the day,
We're struggling on along the way.

Soon from the dear, old home we part,
Although it grieves deep at the heart;
The place we loved in childhood days,
Is tumbling down, and fast decays.

Our whitened locks, and wrinkled brow,
All show how fast we're going now;
We look beyond these fading toys,
And hope to reap eternal joys.

163.
The Grass Will Grow Green.

The grass will grow green after we are all gone,
  For others are coming, after us going,
  And like us, this beautiful world not knowing,
Nor they know not why they so soon follow on.

The grass will grow green after our race is run,
  As millions and millions have gone on before,
  And many more millions are still on the shore,
Coming and going is life under the sun.

The grass will grow green after we are no more,
  When time has outlived us and laid us aside,

In the narrow, lone grave we soon shall abide,
Till God awakes us for the evergreen shore.

The grass will grow green while we sleep in
  the dust.
  No more look out over this beautiful land,
    Where all things are growing, inviting and
      grand;
  The summer's still coming, but then not for us.

The grass will grow green over our quiet home,
  We shall not know, for we shall silently rest
    Beneath the cold ground; we shall still be
      its guest,
  With multiplied millions who this same way
    have gone.

The grass will grow green while we're in our
  low bed;
  We'll gently there rest with the nations now
    past,
  Our bodies lie mouldering, 'neath the green
    grass.
While the flowers are blooming just over our
  head.

The grass will grow green, but O, where shall
  we be?
  Nowhere on this earth can our bodies be
    seen.
  Down in the cold grave, below the grass
    green;
  The birds sing sweetly, but we cannot them
    see.

In the shades of the evening, 'neath the tall bluffs,
  Down in the lone valley green grass will be seen,
  With all else growing so beautiful and green,
But then, not for us, O, then not for us.

The grass will grow green, but, O Lord, Thou dost know,
  How often 'twill grow up to fade and to die,
  Along with humanity, who, too, passeth by;
Coming and going is life here below.

The grass will grow green until time is no more;
  But poor mortals created and placed on the wheel,
  That time is still turning as man doth the reel,
Go onward and onward to the evergreen shore.

164.
Speak Softly.

Softly speak, choose kind words to say,
  For harsh ones will not do;
You'll find it much the safest way,
  Let all this way pursue.

Angry words like thunderbolts,
  Shake up the stillest heart;
They break the tender cords in two,
  And make the feelings smart.

O do not let your passions rise,
   Use gentle words and true;
For angry ones we do despise,
   When milder words will do.

Soft words will safely pave the way,
   For brighter days ahead;
Please use soft words to us today,
   Don't wait till we are dead.

With melting words upon your lips,
   Lit up with a pleasant smile,
You'll shine like polished silver tips,
   If you are free from guile.

Don't wait till we are in our grave,
   For soft, kind words to say;
'Tis now your pleasant words we crave,
   Say soft, kind words to-day.

If the heart is sore, sick and faint,
   Kind words will help to heal;
They'll drive away the worst complaint,
   If love among them steal.

A bitter tongue is like a sting,
   That bites into the flesh;
But kind words help to heal the wounds,
   And start us on afresh.

Kind words, kind words do not forget,
   Father, mother and child;
Kind words are words you'll not forget,
   Then be cheerful, kind and mild.

With ugly looks and angry words,
    Great clouds will gather fast;
Kind words will drive them all away,
    And hide them in the past.

O do not let ill words assail,
    Your neighbor's name deface,
It will no good to you avail,
    Let kind words take their place.

If spite is on the ready tongue,
    Gild it with kind words, pray,
For people now you live among,
    Need kind words every day.

If ugly words be in your heart,
    Find pleasant ones to say,
And bid the ugly ones depart,
    'Tis much the smoothest way.

O speak kind words to one and all,
    At home or in the throng;
Speak soft, kind words to great and small,
    Let kind words be your song.

165.   12s. 8s.

Where Shall Wisdom Be Found.

Iron is taken from the bowels of the earth,
    And brass is molten from the stone;
But as for man, in His wisdom, God putteth no
        trust,
    In none of the works He hath done.

There is a vein in the earth for the brass,
   And a place where gold they can find;
But man has no power by his wisdom, alas!
   To open the eyes of the blind.

From the bowels of the earth come our drink and our bread,
   But its center is yet all on fire;
But who is there can give life and breath to the dead,
   Or raise his poor spirit up higher?

No mountain there is, either of corals or of pearls,
   Can compare to wisdom in love;
Neither gems of bright crystals or costly fine jewels—
   Its price is yet far above.

Seeing 'tis hid from the eyes of the living,
   And kept close from fowls of the air,
Though destruction and death to all are here given,
   This bright jewel is lasting and fair.

There is none but our God who understandeth its ways,
   He seeth from beginning to end;
The course of the winds, and all nature obeys,
   And He bids the rain to descend.

But it is a path that no fowl ever knoweth,
   And the vulture's eye hath not seen;
And the whelp of the lion thereon never goeth,
   It leads to the land of a King.

Who is it that cutteth out rivers in the rocks?
  Bindeth the floods from overflowing?
Or directeth the lambs to the Shepherd of flocks,
  By that unseen path all are going?

By wisdom man knoweth not the worth of it now,
  'Tis bought nor sold by those who're living;
Not Ophir's gold, nor silver one moment allow,
  Nor onyx in change can be given.

Where, O where, then, shall wisdom, true wisdom, be found?
  Or place for the loved ones to roam?
When the dead shall arise and come forth from the ground,
  Ascending to their heavenly home?

Then, O then, there shall wisdom, true wisdom, be found,
  In mansions of wisdom above;
All honor, glory and praise to God shall redound,
  For a home in that city of love.

166.   8s. 7s.

The Good Old Ship of Zion.

Safely sailing o'er the ocean,
  Grand old ship of Zion's King,
Bearing poor, devoted children—
  All are safely borne to Him.
Every heart is filled with gladness,
  Every tongue in songs employ,

Every hour of gloom and sadness,
   Turned into the sweetest joy.

The Lord remembers Zion's children,
   While on the dark ocean's tide,
And moves the good old ship of Zion,
   It safely o'er the waters glides.
Many days and weeks we're sailing,
   O'er the cloudy, misty sea,
But we trust the Lord is guiding
   All along the dangerous way.

One star only is on her banner,
   Only one is in command,
Only one; that's her great leader,
   And with Him we'll safely land.
In the hour of greatest peril,
   He is speaking words of cheer,
And when the night is dark and fearful,
   Every word we gladly hear.

Glorious ship of Zion's children!
   Shouting pilgrims on their way,
All will reach their destination,
   Their great leader all obey.
When we've crossed the dangerous ocean,
   With the voyage safely done,
There'll be lasting consolation,
   Around heaven's great white throne.

Glorious things await His children,
   Soon their journey will be o'er,
When they reach the port called heaven,
   When they touch that sinless shore.

There they'll find sweet songs of welcome,
Shouting millions 'mong the blest,
Countless thousands singing anthems,
Round that sparkling place of rest.

167.   **11s.**

He Careth for You.

Dear children of Jesus, O come, do obey,
The Lord in His goodness forever doth say;
And ever remember your Savior's command,
Inviting and bidding, extending His hand.

He loveth and feedeth true soldiers for Him,
The Lord in His goodness shows mercy to them;
His mercy and favors, He keepeth in store,
And through His great kindness, He dealeth out more.

He remembers His people and careth for them,
And in His great goodness redeemed them from sin;
He remembers His children wherever they're found.
His love and His mercy doth ever abound.

His kindness and blessings do ever appear,
The Lord in His goodness doth speak words of cheer;
The arms of Jehovah, about Israel wound,
Protecting His people in mercy are found.

How happy His children who love and obey,
The Lord in His goodness forever doth say;

He loveth, and careth, and calleth them home,
High up in the heavens His children may come.

They'll shout, and rejoice, as the day's dawn
    appears,
And hearken to Jesus, whose voice they will
    hear;
And arising in glory to mansions above,
Prove God and His goodness and eternal love.

168.
The Creation.

One great, wide waste of trackless wilderness,
    Was the broad earth when first created;
When first the dark, lonesome land appeared,
    'Twas all one night and undivided.

One great, vast region of gloomy night,
    The light of day had not yet broken,
And not a living thing was then in sight,
    Not one word had then been spoken.

Not a creeping worm, nor living fowl,
    Moved upon its face with wonder;
No pain nor death was then upon the soil,
    No lightning, storms, or rains, or thunder.

It was a still, quiet, waiting earth,
    God only, its doom then knowing;
A great, living world was to come forth,
    But then no plant or shrub was growing.

There stood great hills high above the streams,
    Great bleak mountains, tall and bending;

Most wonderful thought! shall I say dreams?
    The huge monster world was then beginning.

God parted the waters from the land,
    And broke the gloomy night in twain;
And with the winds, the broad earth did fan,
    And sent clouds that brought along the rain.

The sun, moon and stars were made to shine,
    And both heat and cold were given;
O how wise and well the trackless line,
    How wisely all things then were shapen.

All gilded by omnipotence high,
    With His well matured intention;
With no footprints then beneath the sky,
    And no life on earth to mention.

But at the word of God's great command,
    There came forth wild beasts and cattle;
Which were driven forth over all the land,
    And prepared, they were for battle.

Then the man, Adam, was given life,
    Placed in charge of all His pasture,
And then Eve was given for his wife.
Both possessed with earthly nature.

Both with their natural life went forth,
    With God's special, good direction;
Although He knew their actual worth,
    Their value and their discretion.

They both went forth like a tender vine,
    Perhaps with their good intention;

But if they should cross a certain line,
   They would meet with sure rejection.

Then they wandered across the deadly path,
   And their joys were then all blighted,
For death and sorrow then held them fast,
   They were no longer with God united.

Now if we could view the world to come,
   Lit up with all its shining beauty,
The kingly place of the Holy One,
   And with everyone on duty.

We would not be curious then to know
   All about this great creation,
For we would then realize God's power,
   Both on earth and up in heaven.

Every page of life would then unfold
   The will, the purpose, and the power,
O'er all the earth, let it still be told,
   That God rules the day and the hour.

169.
Great Mystery.

Great mystery of all mysteries!
   Most mysterious things we see.
The living world, every creature!
   Look at ourselves, what are we?

The blood goes rushing through our veins,
   And the air it feeds our lungs;
Great mystery how this life begins,
   How natural life on earth begun.

How strangely made is everyone,
   Each hair upon our head that grows,
And every creeping thing we see,
   And every worm and fowl that moves.

There's not one bobble or one balk,
   In truth, we know this can be said;
The great, tall tree and little oak,
   How wonderfully they all are made.

The lilac differs from the rose,
   Also the orange from the pine;
The little twig by its brother grows,
   But clusters differ on the vine.

No two alike; how can it be?
   So wonderful are all arranged;
The rivers and all winding streams,
   The great, high mountains, hills and plains.

How curious we are to comprehend,
   The mysterious works ordained;
And all the natural must depend
   On the one, great, creative hand.

The first form was not made by man,
   Neither had he one word to say;
When the great structure was first begun,
   Man was silent, like the clay.

The mystery of all mysteries!
   Creation's work without a flaw;
Science fails to fathom the hidden plan,
   Or light and wisdom from it draw.

Man sinks in darkness with the sun,
  He must wait for the morning light;
He dare not with his own wisdom run,
  Or search for knowledge in the night.

The coming day will all reveal;
  Uncover all great mysteries;
Then we shall know, and will believe
  In God, and know of all his victories.

170.
Heaven.

'Twas one bright, sunny morning in the month of June,
  While sitting beneath a shady bower,
  Meditating during a lonely hour,
Alone, beneath the tall trees before it was noon.

Thoughts came to me more serious than tongue can tell;
  They came floating across my mind so clear;
  Of another life beyond this one drear,
An everlasting life where we'd forever dwell.

But then, where is it? and how far from us away?
  A great, dazzling throng clothed in spotless white,
  In shining garments, grandeur and delight,
A dim vista of life beyond, a coming day.

But is there not a great gulf between us and there?
  Separating us from its great, high wall?

Our bodies the gulf, and soon they must fall.
Only frail bodies of flesh. we should not de-
    spair.

Yes, these mortal bodies will soon cease to
    exist,
  Death's cold. icy hand will take them away;
  The much dreaded band, too, in truth we'll
    say,
But its power and time, there's not one can
    resist.

But then we'll inherit our great heavenly home,
  With its streets of gold and broad fields of
    green,
  Forever in beauty will there be seen,
Where only the righteous are permitted to come.

This world when consumed, the earth purified
    by fire,
  The smoke of the wicked high up ascend,
  Upward, upward, forever without end;
This earth will then be more beautifully attired.

O then, this beautiful earth forever our home;
  Purified and cleansed for the timeless time,
  Delightfully pleasant the same place find,
Where none but the righteous are permitted
    to come.

171.   C. M.
The Dangerous Journey.
We're born, and live, and die in sin,
  'Tis sin on every day.

How we could help our being so,
　I shall not attempt to say.

The law is neither in the heart,
　Or put into the mind,
But we are prone to do our part,
　Our natures bad inclined.

The road is blazed, the way made clear,
　But O, we can't perform!
Our little boat we cannot steer,
　Safely through all the storm.

We follow close and hug the shore,
　And watch the waves go by;
We feel too weak to row across
　The surging waters high.

At last we view a spot of green,
　Beyond the raging flood;
We look, and oh! a hand is seen,
　The guiding hand of God.

An eye of faith beholds a place,
　Where dangers never come;
We look and see the power of grace,
　That takes us to our home.

172.
God's Handiwork.

We should think, when we come to consider the vastness and the greatness of the wonderful and magnificent construction, and mysterious working of all the whole planetary system, arranged so skillfully as to roll on for millions of years, perhaps, and more, without interfering with each other, it ought to convince anyone of the existence of some great Supreme Being who holds the destiny of all in His own hands alone. It would be a preposterous and ridiculous thought to conclude that all these mysterious worlds came into existence, and move onward and onward in their course just as it happens and no collisions ever occur. All go on revolving, round and round, to light up and warm the earth, assisting the earth to feed and support us, and yet man is not willing to give the credit where it belongs, or admit the existence of a good, gracious and all-wise Creator and Controller of the whole entire universe, a one, true and living God, who holds all up and in place by His great, omnipotent power.

The moon shines bright through all the night,
    Among the lonesome trees;
How soft and pure its glimmering light,
    How soft the summer breeze.

The stars they shine so far away,
    Like little specks of gold;
Their beauty, who can half portray,
    Or hath their grandeur told?

The sun divides the day and night,
    Warms up and lights the earth;

It clothes the sky in azure bright,
　　Fills the earth with joy and mirth.

Arranged by one great, skillful hand,
　　So as not to interfere;
All sailing in their orbits grand,
　　Their track is always clear.

Although revolving round and round,
　　A million years or more,
There are no obstructions ever found,
　　And none their path explore.

Alone they ride the trackless waste,
　　Their onward course pursue,
Out in the broad and endless space,
　　Their life is always new.

They never wear themselves away,
　　Nor leave their long fixed sphere,
But still roll on from day to day,
　　And on from year to year.

There's only one whose power they know,
　　Just one who gives command,
By that one power alone they go,
　　By Him alone they stand.

173.　　　　　　　　　　　　　S. M.

Love.

　　Love warms the Christian's breast,
　　　　It soothes and reconciles,
　　Confirms and strengthens confidence,
　　　　And tears are changed to smiles.

Love is our faithful friend,
  In troubles or distress;
It calms and guards us to the end,
  And brings us happiness.

Without it all is loss,
  The sun no longer shines;
This world would be but worthless dross.
  If we no love could find.

'Twould be a raging sea,
  A cold and restless stream;
Resistless would the current be,
  And 'twould with horrors teem.

But God doth move with love,
  And thaws the sinner's heart;
He freely feeds us from above,
  And bids all sin depart.

He leads in pastures green,
  And by still waters sweet;
Our joys, our hopes all flow from Him,
  And happiness complete.

Then let us watch and pray,
  And of all sin repent;
Do all we can on every day,
  To acknowledge mercy sent.

174.   8s. 6s.

Farewell.

Farewell, my Christian friends, farewell,
  At last I bid adieu,

To one and all; O let me tell
    There's rest in heaven for you.

A house all filled with peace above,
    A mansion filled with grace;
A clear, blue sky with shouts of love,
    A shining paradise.

A host, a world of sinners saved,
    Eternal love embraced;
A multitude of heaven-born souls,
    From every earthly place.

Farewell, farewell, at last, farewell,
    I write with tearful eyes.
While here we part, O could I tell
    Of love in yonder skies.

STUBBORNNESS IN THE CHURCH.

How can we restrain our ugly dispositions and stubbornness? They came into this world with us. They grow up with us, they are ours by the gift of nature, and we see no way to entirely uproot them. They are not the most beautiful gifts in the world, but surely they are not proof against reformation. You know you can take a very ugly tree from the forest, plant it in your garden, cultivate and prune it until it will become quite an ornament.

Now, I believe that Christ's people who have these bad streaks of nature, which all inherit, some more, some less, can govern and control their stubbornness and selfishness until there will not be enough left to cause any serious trouble in the church. But it will require an effort. We must be on our guard if we would make a safe voyage, not desiring to cause any disturbance.

We must be like the pilot on the watchtower, always on the lookout. If we are not, we are liable to slide off to one side, among the drift, where there is danger of losing our lives.

If troubles arise in a church and a brother becomes offended at another and is not willing to surrender to better judgment, will not yield to entreaties from faithful brethren, will not carefully watch over his own acts, but treasures up malice against another, for, perhaps, only a supposed wrong, determined not to give way, saying, perhaps, within himself, "I want my brother to know, I want the church to know, and I want the world to know, that I bow my head to no man" now, such a man is a dangerous man, indeed, and I would be sorry to think that he was a representative member in the house of God. What a shame that he will not try to better govern and control himself and gladly submit to the will and wish of the body.

If he is disposed to overrate himself, imagine that he is better that others, he is liable to do much harm, unless he can be shown and made to feel that he is nothing.

Humbleness is one mark of true Christianity, but I think I know something about the warfare which goes on in the transgressor's breast. There is a fearful conflict, at times, within. But old Adam must be subdued, must be kept under control. We must overcome our bigotry, our selfishly disposed will. I know our old natures are hard to handle. Some are, no doubt, a great deal harder to govern and manage than others; but if we would win the battle we must fight the fight, and we must fight to conquer old satan; if we do not, he will destroy our peace and happiness on this earth, and not only ours, but perhaps many others around us. Therefore, we should be firm, determined to put under the man of sin that looms up so big within us.

If we do not control our ugly, stubborn dispositions they will control us. Often, a very little thing will cause a great disturbance, when with just a little condescension at the start, the shedding of one tear, perhaps, all would be over.

But no, our blood is hot, our wrath is kinkled, our temper boils over, our better judgment gives way, and we will not surrender or give one inch, even if it divides the church and spoils its peace. It is like fire when first kindled in the dry grass, it spreads rapidly in every direction, and soon becomes almost unmanageable, when just one cup of water at the right time would have extinguished it. So with those little clouds that hang over us, not bigger than your hand at the start, which soon develop into a big storm. So I believe it is better for us all, when trouble arises among us, not to wait for it to spread from church to church.

The world, too, will come to join in the fight to help sift the matter, and its friendship might prove our ruin. Instead of putting out the fire, it helps to fan the flame. Now, we ought not to let these things grow and so get harder to subdue, but every member ought to consider himself appointed to work for the peace of the little family. If we feel that a brother has done us a great wrong, perhaps he may feel that we have done him a great wrong, and the probability is that both have erred, but each one watching the other's fault is not able to see his own. Now, do not we know there is no good in any of us except that which is born of God?

Then, knowing these things, why not let the inner man rule? But if our feelings are touched we should at least be willing to pursue a scriptural course—go right to our brother, clothed in the spirit of meekness and love. Go at once before the matter spreads or becomes known. But be sure not to approach him in the wrong spirit; do not go until you can go right. Before we start out to get our brother right we must be sure that we are right ourselves, then we will seldom if ever fail to accomplish good. Brother becomes reconciled to brother, and the peace of the flock is spared.

Oh! there is so much difference where one member is trying to bring his brother to his feet instead of throwing himself down at his brother's feet. Do we not know that the love of peace, coupled with meekness, and with a desire to follow after the footsteps of our Savior, is commendable, not only to the church, but to the world also? We can all see our own imperfections better than others can see them in us, and if we acknowledge them, it will strengthen the tie that binds us together. We must not be on the lookout all the time for some brother's fault, but watch our own selves, and perhaps they will do likewise.

We should not allow ourselves to say harmful things of each other, and that, too, before the world. Don't we know that it will soon reach their ears and they will become offended at us? What we say never loses anything by being told again. The world is already looking with distrust at the meek and humble followers of Jesus, and doubting the genuineness of religion, and there are many good, honest, regenerated people living on the outside, not willing to cast their lot with us on account of our bad behavior. We often wonder why the little vine does not grow faster, not realizing all the time that the fault lies with us.

We must practice what we profess and not fight and quarrel and try to devour each other.

remembering all the time that in holding up our brethren we are holding ourselves up, and binding up and strengthening the house of the Lord. A little flock ought to live so that the world could say no harm of it, for then it would be an inviting place for those who are in search of a peaceful home in which to dwell.

> A little flock that Jesus feeds,
>   Purchased by His own blood;
> He cares for them in all their needs,
>   He is their Savior and their God.
>
> A little family by grace divine,
>   Their sins He bore upon the tree,
> They are His jewels, they shall shine,
>   For them He died on Calvary.

When a little flock comes together they must not expect their preacher to worship God for them. We should all come prepared to join in the service of praise and leave our worldly affairs all at home. If our pastor does not feel in the spirit of preaching, we can all talk some, we can tell our experiences and trials along the journey, and speak words of comfort to each other.

We shall not be here long, we are living in a land of uncertainties, our temporal bodies are very frail at best, and we know not how long we shall be permitted to remain in them.

This is no safe, solid resting place for our souls. The sky that looks clear to-day may to-morrow look dark and lowering.

We are living in God's world, and we are His people. We are subject to Him, not Him to us, and we must become reconciled to Him and His will, be willing to submit to His wisdom and way, try to be resigned, prepared and ready to surrender at any moment. The call may come before we are aware, and the flying messenger will come down from heaven, saying, "Child, come home." Then will come the separation. We must then bid farewell to the little band of faithful brethren that we have so often met. When we breathe our latest breath let us hope to be able to give all praise to Jesus, the Lamb of God, which taketh away the sin of the world.

WHAT MUST WE DO TO BE SAVED?

There are two salvations taught in the Bible, one eternal, one temporal. I will try to direct your mind, dear reader, to both, and how they are obtained. If you are an earnest enquirer about your eternal salvation, I would tell you to call on God and not on man. It is not needful to call on man for his assistance, or in any way depend on his puny arm. No man can help you to be born again. God does not require any help to perfect His design. The first law given man he failed to keep and has proven himself a failure ever since.

Would his Creator be likely to intrust to him a matter of so much greater importance—the eternal salvation of souls? Man may look ever so fair, outwardly, and talk ever so smoothly, and yet he may be like a ravening wolf within, or like graves full of dead men's bones. Then do not waste your time following after them, for spiritual life does not come from them.

No preacher, priest or king can pray your sins away for you, there is no mediator between you and God but Jesus. If you have a feeling desire to be saved, go directly to Him and you will not be turned away empty. All who have discovered their own guilt, and come earnestly seeking and begging, will receive the evidence of pardon.

Remember it was your heavenly Father's spirit that showed you your guilt and led you to Him. It taught you to ask and prompted you to act. It is God who begins the work and reveals Himself to you, a result flowing from redemption, which will be performed until the day of Jesus. Then we should not doubt or fear, for all will be well with us. If we are asking, if we are mourning, if we are crying and begging for mercy, we are just as sure of the inheritance as we are that we are now living upon the earth.

If such characters are not saved, who will be? And if this is not the evidence of life, what is the evidence? We cannot be deceived and should not be misled. Go alone to God in prayer, go often, continue going, go in the morning, go at night, until you feel relieved and made to rejoice in Jesus your Savior. This is what we call religion, and this is the only way that I know anything about obtaining it.

With religion comes faith, belief, hope, repentance, love, and a desire for baptism and to follow the meek and lowly Jesus, and partake of all the ordinances of the church. God has given these graces along with your experience, and with these you can work out your temporal, or common salvation. Remember, you now have the will, the desire to obey. There is not much in these loud professions, but a great deal in possession and practice. We are to be known in this world by our works, in this way can let our light shine. Go to the church for a home that you may shelter under its protecting roof. It is a house of refuge, whose inhabitants are the light of the world, a city that is set on a hill and cannot be hid. Great is the Lord, and greatly to be praised in the city of our God. Beautiful for situation is Mt. Zion, the joy of the whole earth. God is known in her palaces for a refuge. It is a palace of safety, a place for poor, weary man to rest, a banqueting house with a beautiful banner, whose ensign is love, daily unfolding and floating over the inhabitants of this little city. The password through the gates is love.

Come inside, dear one, you are invited to come. You need no money to buy fine apparel, come just as you are. Come in and walk about Zion, and go round about her. "Tell the towers thereof, mark ye well her bulwarks, consider her palaces, that ye may tell it to the generation following, for this God is our God forever and ever. He will be our guide even unto death."—Psa. xlviii. 12-14.

What about these towers, and walks, and bulwarks? What do they represent in the church below? The graces of love, hope, joy, peace and happiness. The greatest of these is love; it is the tallest tower in and around the city, and can be seen the furthest. It prepares all the smaller towers to shine so brightly.

It will conquer our approaching foe, subdue our enemies, it is the greatest friend to man the world has ever known. It was love that brought Jesus into the world to die for man; love brought us all out of our troubles; love is the foundation stone of man's eternal happiness.

We must obey God, we must keep His commandments, and He will bless us. We get the will to do and live—the hungering and thirsting—from Him. Then we should heed the invitation. "The Spirit and the bride say, Come; and let him that heareth say, Come; and let him that is athirst come, and whosoever will, let him take the water of life freely." Let him draw from the wells of salvation and eat of the hidden manna.

It is written that He will give unto every one of us according to our works. Do not remain on the outside to starve and die, there is danger out there. You do not have the same promises out there. Snares and traps are thrown around you, satan will tempt you, he is seeking whom he may devour. The carnal mind and all its natural inclinations have undergone no change whatever. The old, polluted and sinful man is easily led astray. But you are born of the Spirit now and your conscience will suffer if you go wrong and do not obey the divine law.

The Spirit teaches you the right way, submit to it and you are safe. Be governed by it, it will lead you right. It will lead and teach you to shun every appearance of evil. It will lead and direct you to the church.

Some one may say, "I do not know where to go. There are so many churches with so many different beliefs and practices"

Well, that is no excuse. You have your Bible, read that. And you have your experience, what does that teach you? Go to the one that comes nearest to following the tracks of the apostolic churches; go to the one that discards all unscriptural practices; go to the one that preaches your experience; go to the one that believes in, and teaches and preaches only the "one Lord, one faith and one baptism;" go to the one that believes only in Christ as the only way, the truth and the life. There is only one way, only one that is right, go there. Go where the members are all humble-minded, where one is not above another, where they do not practice formalities in their worship.

But if the worship of God is in any way connected with pride, fashion or show, do not go there. Do not go where the poor man is not wanted, or where the poor cannot feel at home. Do not go where they show preference for the man of wealth. The poor, humble beggar may be far better than the man who is richly clad.

> Judge not a man by the clothes he wears,
>   Nor by his high and lofty look,
> But judge him by the fruit he bears,
>   It is so written in your Book.

Don't go to a church where there are big I's and little U's, but where all are one and made to feel as brothers. Jesus preached the gospel to the poor. The Lord's people are a poor and afflicted people. Every true Christian feels poor. He feels his nothingness, his littleness and unworthiness, and consequently feels to be the least of all saints.

You need not hunt the church by name, the name does not make Christians or constitute the church of God. To be called Methodist, Baptist, Christian, or something else, does not prove that we are Christians. Christianity is something higher than a name. It is something deep in the heart—it is love. If we love one another, God dwelleth in us. "Hereby know we that we dwell in Him and He in us, because He hath given us of His spirit."—1 John iv. 13.

Then search for the people who have this testimony. Go to them for a home in which to dwell, where unpretending and unfeigned love prevails.

He has set up His kingdom, or church, on earth for His people, and with a law to govern it. If they refuse and reject His kind offerings they must expect to meet the chastening rod. They must expect punishment in some manner, although He does not willingly chastise, yet He cannot change His law to accommodate man or allow him to go on in sin and wickedness and escape the punishment he deserves.

I would like to impress on the minds of men the great importance of obeying. I know there must be some who are old who have felt grieved from day to day by neglecting to attend to these things. Let me say to all such, Don't postpone. You may be standing in the way of others. You cannot afford to trifle along and fool away your precious time on earth. It is a matter that not only concerns you, but your children and your children's children. They may be waiting and watching your action. You can step out from the world and take your place in the church, and the church will be made stronger and the world weaker by your doing so. You can help hold up the little church, or house of the Lord, it needs your presence. You benefit yourself, increase your own happiness, leave the world better by having lived in it. Honor God, be prepared and reconciled to die.

CRITICISM FROM THE WORLD.

How often do we hear the people of the world say, "I wouldn't do the way they do. How can that member of the church be a Christian and live and do the way he does? I make no profession of religion and I know I would not do as they do and say things that they say about each other. And I never could see how they can love and fellowship each other and at the same time be constantly talking about one another. I believe such ones ought to be expelled from the church. I do not think much of a church that will hold such members in fellowship when their daily walk and talk does not begin to compare with the worldlings around them. If they are Christians, we are all Christians," etc.

Now hold. I have heard your complaints and charges, and as a poor, unworthy member, I have a few things to say in reply. Your charges may be true, and if so, I am sorry that such is the case. I know I do not desire to try to defend anyone's ugly ways or misbehavior. But I do have a desire to try to defend the true Christian religion, and try to show that the worldly actions of professors do not always prove them to be hypocrites, and only wearing religion as a cloak to hide away their bad conduct.

Of course we know that all members should keep themselves unspotted from the world. They should not do the way that some one has said of them, they should not disgrace their calling. They should not leave a stain on the fair name of the church of God, or bring a reproach on the other members, and on all truly religious persons everywhere. Such unruly and unguarded members ought to be rebuked in a scriptural and spiritual way, with meekness and humbleness, and cautioned about such things in a way that will not offend.

But now, there are some other things to be considered along here. We must remember that there is not one that liveth and sinneth not. This includes you and I as well as the unruly members spoken of, and you say that you would not do the way they do. Well, perhaps you would not and do not. But now I want you to look over your past and present life carefully, and tell us the truth on yourself, so we may see how clear you are of wrong things, you, who are more than willing to bring accusations against poor members and point out their faults to others.

Yes, you, yourself, may be guilty of doing things that these very ones whom you are talking about would not do. You may be guilty of greater crimes than they. Now, the fact is, we are all guilty of violating the heavenly teachings. Yes, even true Christians cannot and do not at all times, overcome their worldly natures so as to live as they ought to live, and as they are expected and required to live. Their evil natures are just the same as yours and mine, only theirs may crop out in one way and yours and mine in some other way. But of course, we notice the bad conduct of members a great deal quicker than we do that of those who have made no profession, consequently they ought to be all the more careful and watchful over their own actions, doings and sayings before the world, for they are expected to be patterns of morals and good examples for others to follow.

But these accused members may be able to see their own faults to their own sorrow, and deeply repent and regret such things themselves, while you may go on sinning and transgressing daily and not be conscience striken. Here, then, is a vast difference between you and them. They see their sins and are all the time repenting, while you are not able to see yours and never repent, while you are equally as guilty as they.

But if you are conscience stricken and are daily repenting, feeling the weight and burden of sin, then you are a Christian yourself. If this is your condition, you are still behind, for there is a duty resting on you that you have neglected and refused to discharge. Now, your place, too, is in the church, where, perhaps, you might do some good in controlling unruly members. Go at once and acknowledge your imperfections, that you are the vilest of the vile, for these are the feelings of all true Christians.

But do not go and tell how good you are and how bad others are. If you do, the church will not receive you. You must feelingly acknowledge your own sinfulness, expressing a desire to live at the feet of the least. This is the way these unruly members have all done, and this is the way you have not done. You show by your actions that you are ashamed to publicly acknowledge your Lord and Master and the One who stands as your surety before the beautiful gates of paradise. But you stand back and point the finger of scorn at some poor brother who is unable, perhaps, to live and practice the things required of him. Perhaps, if you were filling your place well, you could assist him along a great deal over the uneven places of life's tempestuous voyage.

We are commanded to bear one another's burdens. This can best be done when we are all living together as a spiritual family in love. I am not writing to uphold the unruly and ugly ways of members, for it certainly is to be regretted that we cannot all live so that the world cannot prefer charges against us. May we all try to let our light shine before the world that they may not say harmful things of us. May the grace of God help us to overcome the evil with good, and may we all try to put in practice that which we know to be right, that we may not disgrace our calling and bring reproach on the church, then our little home will be an enjoyable place for others. "Let every one that nameth the name of Christ depart from iniquity. But in a great house there are not only vessels of gold and of silver, but also of wood and of earth; and some to honor and some to dishonor. If a man therefore purge himself from these, he shall be a vesssel unto honor, sanctified and meet for the Master's use, and prepared unto every good work."—2 Tim. ii. 19-21.

OLD AND YOUNG.

I once was young, but now I am old. I am now almost a contsant sufferer, though I should not complain, for God has been good to me, far better than I deserve. I cannot and do not hope for anything better in this life than the past has brought me, although it has been a thorny way. I have drank of the bitter waters, my cup has been full and running over. I have met with many disappointments, and trials and sorrows have traveled the road with me.

The things that were once inviting to me have no charms now. Air castles and finely painted pictures of this world's promises do not shine before my eyes now. I cannot see much in the short journey ahead that would add to my enjoyment. All the glittering toys of life are fast fading away with me. The fair promises that lead the young on so hopefully have vanished and gone. I can now say, "Vanity of vanities." The sun has far passed the meridian with me and must soon set behind the hill.

Well, when I come to look around and view my surroundings, what do I find left for one like myself? Is there nothing for my poor soul to feed upon during my short stay?

Most certainly there is. Then I will not despair, no, not for one moment. There is the family tie, and the many warm friends who are so near and dear to me. But I know I am not much longer to see their friendly faces here; I must soon give them all up and take the last farewell. Then, last but not least, is my hope of heaven. Can I not look beyond the dark curtains of this poor, fading world? Can I not see the light of that better life that is coming?

Life here is only in the bud that is to break forth in that clear and cloudless sky above, a full grown, ripe flower, that is to bloom on and on, sending forth its sweets throughout one long and unending eternity.

Yes, hope springs up and brightens as we grow older. The much dreaded old age then need not be the darkest days of life's journey, for we can now look into the future with a great deal of satisfaction and draw comfort from its promised happiness.

I desire to be ready at any time to surrender to the last call, and I do hope we shall meet all the dear loved ones of earth again over on the other side of death's angry stream, just across the cold river, on the beautiful shores where parting will be no more forever.

When I was young, it was so different from now. I hardly realized that I ever would grow old; it seemed so far away from me, only a faint glimmering sight in the then, seemingly, far away future. Sometimes, but only for a moment, would I gaze ahead, my mind was so completely wrapped up in the perishable things of this world. Although I could see the aged tottering to and fro as if they could scarcely walk, yet this I could not bring home to myself. But while I was drifting along age was creeping upon me. When meditating, sleeping or laboring, I was being carried along. No matter where I was or what the engagement, it was the same, I was constantly growing older, time was fast hastening me on.

In those days I verily thought happiness depended on how much of this world's goods I could get together. It was a gay and inviting world to me. Often my pursuit would bring thorns and thistles, but inspired by hope I was led on step by step—there was no letting up. Again and again I would plunge along and as often be overtaken with misfortune. But I would form new resolutions and press on for the much coveted prize and before I hardly knew that old age was approaching, it was upon me, it had over taken me while I was so busily engaged fighting the battles of life. I can hardly realize now that what seemed so far away in my young days is now resting upon me. I now see the summers and winters go by at a more rapid pace than ever. The flowers bloom in the spring, the green leaves put forth on the trees and but a little while and all are gone.

Now I desire to say a few words to those who are young at the present time. Before you are aware of it old age will come; none can escape if permitted to live. Your young days will soon be passed.

Would you take advice from one who has traveled over the road that you are now going? There are many crooks and turns and unthought-of paths to lead from the safe way and take you along the road to ruin, which, sooner or later, will land you in disgrace and shame.

Would you live happy here in this short life? Then lend a helping hand to others. If you would, then study to know the right and practice it; to know the wrong and forsake it. Shun the evil that surrounds you, that you may escape the poison that might, sooner or later, ruin you, and not only you, but might leave its black mark upon your innocent family and their posterity. Would you leave a curse, a sting, a reproach that would follow them to their graves? If you would not, then shun every appearance of evil. "Resist the devil and he will flee from you."

If your parents have set good, moral examples before you, follow them, do as they direct and you are safe; but if they have not, then set good examples for them.

I once knew a man who told me he went into a saloon to take a drink. He said he thought his son was going with him, but on entering he looked back and saw his son leaving with his head cast down. Right there he said he formed a resolution, that hereafter he would try to set good, moral examples before his children, instead of them having to set examples for him, and from that day he never again visited the dramshop, but became its most bitter and active enemy.

Right here let me warn all young men to flee from that low, degraded place, shun it as you would an adder—the devil's active companion on earth. It has spoiled the peace of millions, and millions of homes have been swept away by it, whole families wrecked and degraded. It has left more people destitute and distressed than all other crimes put together. I have known those around us brought down to ruin by it, left paupers and vagabonds upon the earth, without home or shelter, clothed in starvation and rags, who in their troubles resort to crime and finally land in prison, and at last fill a grave in disgrace.

Drinking fathers bring all this on their poor, heart-crushed families.

Then, young man, it is very necessary sometimes for you to set good examples before your father and try to save him. And if you really desire to see good days and be happy, lead a quiet and happy life and form no bad habits. They are so easily formed and so hard to break up. If you wish to make life a success and have all good people love and esteem you, do not drink, do not gamble, do not visit secret places where you would not be willing for your best friend to see you, do not chew tobacco or use wicked oaths, trying to please and keep up with your associates. It may look smart to some, but it does not to others, and it will bring you no lasting happiness, but only makes you look silly and ignorant to those who do differently and have had better training.

You may cause reflection on the good morals of your parents and you ought to have more respect for them and their good name. Select your company as you would your food or your clothing. But when your lot is cast with the evilly inclined, treat them well, and if you can reform them by good and kind words, do so. Lookout for traps and snares and many temptations all along the way—beautifully painted signs in disguise to capture and lead the silly and unsuspecting ones to ruin. A step here and one there on the right and on the left, either way, perhaps, will lead to vice and crime. Seek to do and practice that which is right and good in the sight of those who are good and thereby build up for yourself a good name and character in the world which is worth more to a young man than gold. Build up a reputation for truthfulness, honesty, industry and economy, with good moral habits, and take my word for it, this you will never regret.

Always pay your just and honest debts, try to treat others as you would have them treat you and this will bring you a rich reward, a peaceful and perhaps long life, where plenty and pleasure abound.

But the other way brings hunger, discontent, rags, and sometimes the jail. A great deal depends on getting started right. Make yourself contented with such things as you have, make your every-day surroundings pleasant, try to be satisfied with your condition and lot, whatever it may be.

Dear children, listen to these things, try to forsake the wrong and cling to the right. You will soon find that old age is creeping upon you, too. Some day you may have the Lord's precious pearl hid away in your bosom and then there will be an incentive to live and practice a Christian life. All these things will add to your enjoyments on earth, and certainly will not rob you of heaven.

LOVE.

Religion is love. It comes from God. We should always remember that God is love, and without love we could not truthfully claim to be His children. Love is not a merchantable something, bought and sold, or dealt out by the slight and cunning of men. It is not a gift from man to man, but is born in one's own breast, a welcome guest in the bosom of poor, fallen creatures. Where love dwells there is a heart full of repentance, a godly sorrow for every sin committed. This is the result of the tender workings of love. If we are born of God we must be like Him, bear His image. He first loved us, we must love Him in return, must love His children, must love all His works, love to obey His law, love good deeds, hate wickedness. Love and hatred are bitter enemies. One is the child of God, the other the child of the devil. The two cannot dwell together in peace, there is always a warfare.

Dear one, do you know anything about this warfare? If you do, you are a Christian, a child of God, and your soul is filled with his love. Stay with him, live for him, shelter under his wings, for he loves his own and his protecting arm is extended around his people who walk humbly before him. He will not forsake them nor turn a deaf ear to their cry. Love seeketh to do good, is easily entreated. The opposite to love is hate, bold, defiant, daring and destructive. Love is pure and gentle and leadeth one on after God's commandments in the path of duty, with faith in the righteousness of our dear Lord and Master. One of his humble followers is a lover of his glorious truth, has no bad designs or evil intentions, is not puffed up and filled with bigotry, loves his neighbors, loves the church, the preacher and the gospel, loves the brethren, and is willing to help bear their burdens. Love teaches and leads him to assist the poor and needy ones, remembers the troubled ones and cares for the sick ones.

If a man is found hungry, love feeds him; if he is a stranger in the cold world, love comforts him and finds shelter for him. Love is an unfading flower that never dies. We cannot be robbed of its beauty nor its usefulness. It is a living plant, and its future home is in the skies. All the costly and shining ornaments of this poor world sink out of sight when compared to love. It is a sweet and tender blossom that will continue to bloom on and on until it ripens in heaven. It makes no enemies on earth and has none in heaven. It will tame wild beasts, subdue reptiles, drive out wicked thoughts, control our ugly natures and make them look respectable. It is the finger board pointing the way to a peaceable journey ahead, directing the weary traveler, comforting poor, worn-out pilgrims who are taking their last steps on earth, visits the widow and orphan in their afflictions and conducts and guides all along on their journey to their long home beyond the grave.

TIME.

Time travels, comes and goes and never returns. The day we now live and enjoy we shall see no more. The sun that shines today may shine again, but not on this day. The past day is gone forever to us. Today we live, others die; tomorrow we die, others live. Our bodies grow up of existing material. There is no new created material, but a development according to a purpose and law, a changing from one form to another. Forms may perish and decay, but the decaying matter has not lost its usefulness. So the world of living creatures move. Bodies come and go. Time develops bodies—time takes them away. Bodies do not move nor change the mission of time. The earth will continue to revolve with its load of living substance and material properties. Earth, air and water are full of life. Time sweeps all on its great current. Finally, all natural life will perish, according to purpose and arrangement, but time will still continue. And so will that which is spiritual. The spiritual never dies, but will be separated from all that is natural. The spiritual needs no cleansing for it is already pure. It could not be otherwise, originating and coming from God. Corruption and incorruption cannot long exist together. They are no more alike than darkness and light. The high hand of Providence directs all changes. No life has power to change itself into some other kind of life different from the one it possesses. Life brings life only like itself. Life comes and goes but there is always an origin. Life cannot bring itself into existence, nor can it exist without permission and purpose. Man creates nothing, he is the created, that is all. But the great unseen moves on with its wonderful and mysterious developing, bringing life upon the stage of action, and taking it away. The great, strong wheels of time will continue to move and roll on, crushing everything before it. Nothing can stop or hinder its course. It will not fail to accomplish the purpose of the great, all-wise Supreme Being. All will conform strictly to his will and in the end we hope to find all things are for the best.

THE GOSPEL PREACHER.

The effect produced by the preaching of the gospel depends a great deal on the way it is presented. Ministers can give to congregations their view of the Bible questions, but it should be in a very gentle, meek and child-like manner, that is, if they desire and expect good results. The preacher never can accomplish much good by abuse, harsh words or remarks that would in any way offend or wound the feelings of those that hear. Man is disposed to believe what he does believe whether right or wrong, and he will not let loose quickly his opinions and fall in with yours. Although you may be presenting Bible truth he will not change and accept it. He must have something presented that is in harmony with his own way of thinking, in accord with his own established views.

Men are not convinced of their wrong by any little whiff that comes along. They require plenty of time to study and reflect over what they have heard. If they find that the Bible sustains your view after awhile some may accept and believe your teaching to be correct. But even then there a great many who may be so filled with prejudice that they will not allow themselves, no matter how plainly the facts are stated, to believe. The only way to succeed reasonably well with such ones, in my opinion, is to court their affections in every day life, get their confidence built up in you, get them to esteem and love you. A minister can then accomplish some good. His every-day life must be a pattern in good morals. His character should be without a stain. He must never be known to tell an untruth. If he should, it certainly would ruin his usefulness. But after he has once established himself as a man of truth, virtue, honesty and earnestness, earned and gained the confidence of the people, then he can present the gospel truth with some show of success. He can take his Bible and read and comment on its teachings, give his views and ask the people to compare them with the scriptures. He can explain with firmness and men after awhile will begin to investigate, and now and then one or more will drop their own views and fall in with his, a little now and a little then, until they are fully established in the faith and doctrine of the Bible. But some never can be converted from a wrong, their traditions binding them to an error through life. It is not in accord with their human nature to believe that some one else is nearer right than they are, and not only so, if they were convinced, they would never admit the fact, it would be too much condescension for their bigoted and selfish dispositions. But the true servant of the Lord must be humble minded, not puffed up, not desirous of making a show in the world, to show himself to good advantage; but just be plain and simply what he is, not attempting to go beyond lest he fall far below. Every man should be satisfied when he fills his own place and not try to fill some other man's place. If another has a better gift than you, then you ought to be pleased to hear him and not be jealous of his gift, fearing that he might stand higher among the brethren than you. We ought to remember that all gifts come from the Lord and that all are profitable in their place, but out of their place they become useless. Then how careful all ought to be in trying to find out where they belong, in order that they may accomplish some good for the Lord's people, no matter whether it be head or foot. If it is the Lord's will we ought to be reconciled and willing to work where he has called us.

SONGS OF PRAISE AND PRACTICAL LIFE.

175.   8s. 7s.
Who Will Speak the Most Cheering Words?

O, I'm growing old and tired,
  And my form is stooped and bent;
Who'll stand by me in the evening
  And will make my soul content?

Who will cheer me on my journey
  While my eyes are growing dim?
Who will comfort me and cheer me
  When I'm facing death so grim?

I'm a poor, wandering pilgrim,
  Feel I've almost lost the trail.
Of my dear and loving Savior,
  And that surely I must fail.

Once across the tiresome journey,
  And a peaceful life begun—
O, that I could reach the haven,
  When my hard day's work is done.

Who will cheer me 'cross the desert,
  Safely to the promised land?
Who will speak the words most cheering,
  And hold up my feeble hand?

Who will cheer me o'er the mountains,
  'Cross the rugged hills and plain,
To a safe and happy landing,
  To a land without a stain?

Who will speak the words most cheering,
  'Long the sun-scorched, heated sands?
Who'll conduct me to the fountain
  'Cross the dried and parched up lands?

Who will guide me o'er the ocean,
  When the waves are rolling high,
Who will speak the words most cheering,
  When at last I'm called to die?

When the last long night is ended,
  Then on whom shall I depend?
Who will speak the words most cheering
  Unless it be my Savior, friend?

176.   S. M.
        Sinner's Low Appeal.
    O wilt thou, dearest Lord,
      Pour in the oil and wine?
    Annoint the sore, afflicted part,
      Of this poor heart of mine.

    O wilt thou hear my cry,
      The sinner's low appeal,

The broken heart that heaves a sigh;
  Wilt Thou all bruises heal?

O, wilt Thou, wilt Thou give
  The aching heart relief?
Let sinners look to Thee and live,
  And take away their grief?

O, wilt Thou hear our prayers?
  And give the weary rest?
Repenting sinners wilt Thou cheer,
And calm their troubled breast?

177.   8s. 7s.

Home.

Soon we'll cross the chilling river,
  Bid the world a last good-bye;
Then we'll reach the long forever,
  Far above the clouded sky.

Soon we'll cross the chilling river,
  To a land that's far away;
Where no storm clouds ever gather,
  In the land of endless day.

Just across the chilling river
  Lies the port we hope to gain;
In the far-off, glad forever,
  Ever there we hope to reign.

Just across the chilling river,
  Where the shining light is seen,
Over to the long forever,
  Ever, ever to remain.

178.   8s. 7s.
Stand By The Truth.

We should not stand on doubtful ground,
   Nor for doubtful points contend;
But place ourselves where truth is found,
   It alone we should defend.

We're not to please ourselves below,
   After no false teachers run;
Against the truth they always go,
   Against the Father and the Son.

179.   L. M.
"Let Not Your Heart Be Troubled."

Let not your heart be terrified,
For you your Savior bled and died;
For you Christ Jesus hath appeared,
And you are numbered and prepared.

Be not afraid, for Christ has said,
"I'll come again and raise the dead;
I'll bring my ransomed children home,
And where I go, there they shall come.

Let not your heart be troubled, then,
For He will surely come again;
High up in heaven your name he'll seal,
And from that court there's no appeal.

O, do not doubt, it was the Lord,
Who loved you and who spake the word;
And "If I go away," he said,
"I'll come again, be not afraid."

Let not your heart be troubled, then,
  Obey your dearest Savior, friend;
Be like a lamb, stay around the fold,
  Where love and peace fill up the soul.

180.   C. M.
Baptized.

I raised my voice to heaven high,
  My mind did soar away;
Then lo! I heard my Savior say,
  "Dear child, dear child, obey."

"Be buried in the liquid grave,
  A token of pure love;"
And thus He spoke to me and said,
  "Your Father is God above."

"Take up thy cross and follow me,"
  The Lord hath truly said;
"Come unto me and I will give
  Thee everlasting bread."

O bright, sweet day, the day of rest,
  Down by the water's side,
There my poor soul was greatly blest,
  For it was satisfied.

181.   C. M.
The Heathen.

God moves in dark and heathen lands,
  Unknown to you and me;
But there He's found with out-stretched hands
  To poor humanity.

Broad as the earth, and wide as space,
  Is God's eternal love,
Dealt out to Adam's fallen race,
  So kindly from above.

All o'er the earth He finds His tribes
  Of every shade and cast;
Jehovah still with them abides,
  And saves them by His grace.

Amongst all the kindred tribes of earth,
  In every hiding place,
His love and power is manifest,
  The tender hand of grace.

182.   P. M.

Ye Must Be Born Again.

When dead in trespass and in sin,
  And by God's sentence slain,
We have no faith to call on Him,
  Till we are born again.
      Ye must be born again,
      Ye must be born again,
We have no faith to call on Him
  Till we are born again.

'Twas sin that brought us all our ills,
  Brought all our aches and pain;
While dead in sin we have no will,
  Till we are born again.
      Ye must be born again,
      Ye must be born again,

While dead in sin we have no will,
  Till we are born again.

The Spirit with its quickening power,
  Hath not one single stain;
It touched my heart and tears flowed out—
  Then I was born again.
    Ye must be born again,
    Ye must be born again,
It touched my heart and tears flowed out—
  Then I was born again.

For sin, my sin, I plainly felt,
  That Christ the Lord was slain,
Then low before my God I knelt,
  When I was born again.
    Ye must be born again,
    Ye must be born again;
Then low before my God I knelt,
  When I was born again.

183.   8s. 6s.

Not Here.

No resting place for us is found,
  'Mongst earthly traps and snares,
No safe retreat or sure repose,
  Or place where rest appears.

Not in life's tempestuous waves,
  Beating around us here;
Not one hope from the surging tide
  Doth yet to us appear.

A night has come, a day is gone,
   Forever with the past;
Why should we care for morning's dawn?
   Or drifting time so fast?

We look away and plainly see
   Just two bright lights ahead,
Among the green and living trees,
   A green spot for our bed.

We cast our eyes beneath the oak,
   Behold, appear just three;
Tired and worn they seem to look,
   While sitting 'neath the tree.

Across the rolling, beating waves,
   Behold a pleasant grove,
Along the distant water's edge,
   A green spot filled with love.

Not here can such a place be found.
   In all this showy land,
No safe retreat the world around,
   No rest for tired man.

184.   8s. 7s.

The Lonely Dead.

So sad and lonely is the spot,
   Where the silent dead are found;
There the wind goes softly whispering
   O'er the loved ones in the ground.

'Tis a melancholy place for me,
   'Mongst the little piled up mounds;

For 'neath the shady, lonesome trees,
  Sleep the dear ones in the ground.

We often go there sad and weeping,
  Where the dearest ones are found,
Where so silently they're resting
  'Neath the cold and chilly ground.

There we stand awhile, reflecting,
  About the friends here strewn around,
Of the dear ones much lamented,
  Who are resting 'neath the ground.

We stand, still looking on with wonder,
  For awhile we feel spell-bound;
Soon shall we be of their number,
  And lie with them 'neath the ground.

May we meet them up in heaven,
  Where no parting tear is found,
And no farewell is ever taken,
  Far above the lonesome ground.

For this we hope, and for this we pray. O, could we but meet all our dear friends beyond their sleeping home in the ground, where no parting tear is shed and no farewells are ever taken.   June 30, 1898.

185.

The Poor, Helpless Cripple.

Before the temple's beautiful gate,
  There sat an impotent man;

Close to the apostles' weary feet,
　　His poor, fainting cry began.

He who begged thus to be healed,
　　Was in this condition born;
Long time he waited help to come,
　　But was of hope almost forlorn.

Look unto us, the apostles said,
　　Faith in God will make you strong;
Jesus Christ is the fountain head,
　　Thus answered Peter and John.

We have no silver, we have no gold,
　　But such as we have we give;
Jesus of Nazareth can make you whole,
　　You must look unto Him and live.

Peter took the poor man by the hand.
　　And raised him up on his feet;
And praising God then at once began,
　　At the temple's beautiful gate.

This same Jesus Christ is set at naught,
　　Though He was the corner stone;
In no other name is salvation wrought,
　　And no other name is known.

There at the temple's beautiful gate,
　　At the apostles' tired feet,
Jesus healed this poor, helpless cripple;
　　His salvation made complete.

186. 8s. 7s.
Who Will Wait.

Who will wait for me at sundown,
    When the clouds are gathering fast.
Darkness spreading over the valley,
    And the silvery moon has passed?

CHORUS:

Who will wait for me at sundown,
    Who will wait for me, who'll wait?
Who will wait for me at sundown,
    When the evening's cold and late?

Who will wait for me at sundown,
    When the day is passed and gone,
When the cold, damp winds are blowing,
    And I'm far away from home?

CHO.—

Who will wait for me at sundown,
    At the closing of the day,
When I feel almost deserted,
    And am lost along the way.

CHO.—

Who will wait for me at sundown,
    When the lamp is burning low,
When the hour is dark and lonesome,
    And my traveling seemeth slow?

CHO.—

If my Savior's found there waiting,
    At the setting of the sun,

When my last, sad breath is parting,
  When my earthly race is run.

CHO.—

  Then, O, then I'll be most happy,
    At the closing of the day;
  I shall never more go tramping.
    'Long the dark and lonesome way.

CHO.—

187.   L. M.

The Young.

The young, the giddy and the proud,
Soon they'll be wrapped in death's cold shroud;
Their pilgrimage will soon be o'er,
Soon they must leave this earthly shore.

The day that now looks bright and clear,
Will soon give place for doubts and fear;
The pains of death will them embrace,
And change their mortal resting place.

The world will offer words of cheer,
But soon its ways looks dark and drear;
The child-like notions fade away,
They're followed by a solemn day.

The brightest pearls from oceans wide,
Or richest gems from mountain's side,
Could not turn the Almighty God,
Nor buy this world for our abode.

O happy thought, O day of joy,
When we are freed from earth's alloy!

The silent twinkling of one star,
Sends grace and beauty from afar.

188.   P. M.
Plea for Mercy.

Great God of all the earth and sky,
   Wonderful things of Thee are spoken,
Both power and wisdom from on high,
   Thy way and will cannot be broken.

And the bound of love is endless space,
   Thy power beyond our comprehension,
And Thy knowledge, too, is unsurpassed,
   Thy course and way without direction.

We're only a mote before Thine eye,
   All nations are but a speck to Thee;
Thou can'st pluck them up and them destroy,
   For so weak and helpless here are we.

We would not divide Thy glory, Lord,
   Would not rob Thee of Thy starry crown;
Would not disbelieve Thy written word,
   Nor any part of it disown.

But we in Thy great creation stand,
   Just one link in the great endless chain,
One link by Thine own creative hand,
   Powerless, too, yet we'd not complain.

We're only before Thee like a straw,
   Carried about by the shifting wind;
We are feeble to obey hy Tlaw,
   With our worldly appetites within.

Knowing our weak and failing ways,
   We would ask protection every hour;

Guard us during all our sinful days,
   And save us from the serpent's power.

O we desire not to ruin to go;
   How feeble we are to do Thy will;
O we cannot help our being so,
   Yet wilt Thou, dear Lord, protect us still.

We fall like poor beggars at Thy feet,
   Great sinners prostrate before Thee lie;
We beg, pray and ask for mercies great,
   Forsake us not when we come to die.

189.
Where Shall Unfailing Rest be Found?

Not along the road to wealth, almost from one's very birth;
Not 'mongst the jangles of a proposed resting place on earth;
Not in wandering from the path of one's understanding,
Nor in life's brightest pages found so charming and enchanting,
               Not there.

Not in the restless world, with its grand and gay deceivings,
Nor 'mongst the unknown written pages of life's sad misgivings,
Nor the enticing pleasures found among the different nations;
Not in journeying with the gay, proud world of fashions,
               Not there.

Not in hard-fought battles with their wrongly
　　formed conclusions;
Not in a dissipated life with many sad delu-
　　sions;
Not in temples made with hands with their
　　vain portals gleaming;
Not in revelry by night where fondest hopes
　　are dreaming.
　　　　　　　　　　　　Not there.

Searching these earthly idols through, no
　　resting place is found;
There is a haven far away and to that place
　　all are bound.
'Tis a place far, far away that no mortal eye
　　hath seen,
A place of rest prepared where no earthly
　　man hath been,
　　　　　　　　　　　　'Tis there.

A city whose builder is God, His everlasting
　　throne,
Its streets are paved with gold, its shining
　　walls of jasper stone;
There we hope some day to dwell, where un-
　　ending rest is found,
In the land of angels where untold love and
　　rest abound—
　　　　　　　　　　　　'Tis there.

INDEX.

POETRY.

	Page.
Am I His Child?..	5
Angels	78
A Prayer	90
Armies of the Living God	95
A Debt of Gratitude to God.	113
A Rotten Ball	128
A Prisoner	25
A Poor Weary Traveler	33
Born Again	26
Before the Church	31
Bear Us Away	39
Be Ye Reconciled	109
Born to Die	132
Baptized	224
City of God	30
Children of God	54
Cheer Up	112
Come to Christ and Drink	145
Church Home	57
Departed Ones	40
Death's Unbroken Chain	85
Desire for Baptism	110
Departed Friends	116
Draw Me Closer	141
Death	142
Death	155
Day is Breaking	146

INDEX.

Experience	14
Experience	147
Experience	153
Ever the Same	61
Each One Must Bear His Part	67
Entangled With the Enemy	70
Erring Sons	133
Flesh and Blood	13
Free Grace	17
Free Grace	32
Fallen Man	60
Flying Hours	79
Follow Him	88
Friendly Home to Come	99
Farewell	182
Gift of Love	18
God's People	34
Gloom of Death	37
God's Banner of Love	39
God Does All	74
Gloom O'ershadows the Mind	85
God's People	87
God Gives the Life	97
Grace Paid it All	103
Gospel Tidings	105
Gospel for All	131
God is Everywhere	151
Great Mystery	175
God's Handiwork	179
Heavenly Canaan	11
His Name	28
Help Us to Pray	29
He Will Save Us	139
He Comes	155
He Careth for You	172
Heaven	177
Heaven	158
Home	222
In Peace	107
In Memory of a Departed Brother	143
In the World	162

INDEX.

Jesus Our Savior	9
Love	6
Last Farewell	22
Lift Us Up	35
Let Love be Ours	38
Love	118
Love	181
Let Not Your Heart be Troubled	223
My Works and Ways	69
My Poor Life	70
My Poor Ways	149
Not Here	226
O Could I Tell	76
Our Delight	102
Our Joys	102
Our Hope	114
Our Gloomy Life	119
Our Desire	122
On the Rolling Wave	144
Our Lustful Eyes	156
Pilgrims in the World	36
Prayer	58
Pain and Sorrow	86
Parental Home	163
Plea for Mercy	232
Religion	12
Religion is Life and Light	68
Remember Ye the Lord	93
Return, Repent	97
Sea of Sin	7
Star of Bethlehem	24
Spiritual Family	50
Sweet to Meet	66
Shall We Hope to Meet Again	80
Song	95
Sing Songs in Praise to God	100
Sheep Abroad	118
Serving Out Our Time	130
Song	136
Speak Softly	156
Stand by the Truth	222
Sinner's Low Appeal	221

INDEX.

The Reaper	2
Thy Way	8
The Heavenly Home	10
The Church's Invitation	16
The Stream of Love	19
This Dreary Life	20
The Way, the Truth and the Life	21
The Grave	28
The World	43
The Suffering Gate	44
The Carnal Mind	45
The Kingdom Shall Stand	47
The Young	51
This Life is Like a Stream	52
The Apostle Paul	53
The Preacher	56
To Concord Association	62
To Die is Gain	64
The Conflict	65
The Gospel Bell	72
Thankfulness	73
The Good Old Way	76
The Lord Knows Our Way	82
The Triune God	83
The Time to Die	84
The Poor, Lone Beggar	86
The Church	89
Thankfulness	90
They are Gathering Home	93
The Bitter Cup	100
The Church	101
The Gospel Plan	104
The Good Old Church	108
The Least	111
The Gospel	115
The Apostle Paul	120
To Be Born Again	123
Thanksgiving Day	124
The Grave	125
The Song of Love	131
The Strait Way	134
'Tis Sweet to Meet	136

INDEX.

The Unseen God 138
The World 140
Thankful 160
The Grass Will Grow Green 164
The reation 173
The Dangerous Journey 178
The Young 221
The Heathen 224
The Lonely Dead 227
The Poor, Helpless Cripple 228

Unregenerated 96

Waiting for the Promised Land 41
Wayside Sinner's Lamentation 47
Weary Not 59
We Come 62
We Would Skip the Hills 63
We Will Pass On 66
We Must Look Beyond 92
Wandering Pilgrim 106
With Christ Above 120
Wandering Children 126
With God 129
We Long for Rest 157
Where Shall Wisdom be Found 168
Went Astray 111
We Must Wait 60
Who Will Wait 224
Where Shall Unfailing Rest be Found 233

You Must be Born Again 225

PROSE.

Page.

Criticism From the World 200

Love 212

Old and Young 205

Stubbornness in the Church 185

Time 215
The Gospel Preacher 217

What Must We do to be Saved 192

www.ingramcontent.com/pod-product-compliance
Lightning Source LLC
Chambersburg PA
CBHW022009220426
43663CB00007B/1014